MathFlare

Name: ______________________

Class: __________

Teacher: ________________________

Introduction

As parents and educators, we recognize the pivotal role mathematics plays in shaping a child's academic journey and future success. Yet, the path to mathematical proficiency can often seem daunting, fraught with challenges and complexities. That's where the transformative power of MathFlare Workbooks shine through, illuminating the way forward with clarity, precision, and purpose.

Introducing MathFlare Workbooks – a beacon of guidance, a testament to excellence, and a catalyst for achievement. Crafted with meticulous care and expertise, MathFlare Workbooks stand as paragons of educational excellence, designed to nurture young minds, ignite a passion for learning, and develop a deep-rooted understanding of mathematical concepts.

Picture this: your child eagerly delves into the pages of Mathflare Workbook, greeted by a step-by-step guide illuminated with vivid examples that demystify complex mathematical concepts. With each turn of the page, they embark on a journey of discovery, encountering thoughtfully curated practice questions that reinforce learning and hone problem-solving skills. And when they unveil the answers to those very questions, a sense of accomplishment blossoms within them – a tangible reward for their hard work and dedication.

But MathFlare Workbooks are more than just tools for learning; they are pathways to comprehension, fostering a deep-seated understanding of mathematical concepts through a sequential, logical flow. From fundamental principles to advanced problem-solving strategies, every chapter builds upon the last, ensuring a robust foundation upon which future knowledge can be constructed.

As parents, we yearn for nothing more than to see our children thrive, to witness the spark of inspiration ignited within them as they conquer academic challenges with confidence and poise. MathFlare Workbooks serve as partners in this noble endeavor, offering not just practice questions, but the keys to unlocking a world of opportunity.

And for teachers, MathFlare Workbooks stand as invaluable allies in the quest to cultivate mathematical proficiency in the classroom. With answers readily available, instructors can focus on guiding and nurturing their students, confident in the knowledge that MathFlare Workbooks provide a solid framework upon which to build.

In the pages of MathFlare Workbooks, we find not just the promise of academic excellence, but the seeds of a brighter tomorrow. So let us embrace the power of mathematics, let us champion the journey of learning, and let us pave the way for a generation of young minds poised to shape the world. With MathFlare Workbooks as our guide, the possibilities are infinite, and the future, bright.

Table of Contents

MathFlare
Grade 2
MATH WORKBOOK
Step by Step Guide and Essential Practice with Answers
Addition Subtraction
Multiplication
Place Value and Expanded Notations
Geometry
MathFlare Publishing

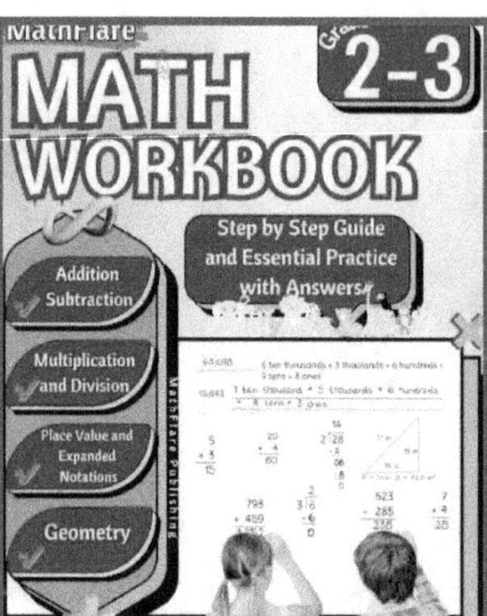
MathFlare
Grade 2-3
MATH WORKBOOK
Step by Step Guide and Essential Practice with Answers
Addition Subtraction
Multiplication and Division
Place Value and Expanded Notations
Geometry
MathFlare Publishing

MathFlare
Grade 3
MATH WORKBOOK
Step by Step Guide and Essential Practice with Answers
Multiplication and Division
Decimals
Place Value and Expanded Notations
Fractions and Geometry
MathFlare Publishing

MathFlare
Grade 1
MATH WORKBOOK
Step by Step Guide and Essential Practice with Answers
Counting and Numbers
Addition and Subtraction
Place Value and Expanded Notations
Understanding Time
MathFlare Publishing

MathFlare
Grade 1-2
MATH WORKBOOK
Step by Step Guide and Essential Practice with Answers
Counting and Numbers
Addition and Subtraction
Place Value and Expanded Notations
Understanding Time
MathFlare Publishing

MathFlare
Grade 3-4
MATH WORKBOOK
Step by Step Guide and Essential Practice with Answers
Addition Subtraction
Multiplication Division
Place Value and Expanded Notations
Fractions and Geometry
MathFlare Publishing

MathFlare
Grade 4
MATH WORKBOOK
Step by Step Guide and Essential Practice with Answers
Addition Subtraction
Multiplication Division
Place Value and Expanded Notations
Fractions and Geometry
MathFlare Publishing

MathFlare
Grade 4-5
MATH WORKBOOK
Step by Step Guide and Essential Practice with Answers
Multiplication Division
Place Value and Expanded Notations
Fractions and Geometry
Unit Conversion
MathFlare Publishing

MathFlare
Grade 5
MATH WORKBOOK
Step by Step Guide
and Essential Practice
with Answers
Multiplication Division
Place Value and Expanded Notations
Fractions and Geometry
Unit Conversion
MathFlare Publishing

MathFlare
Grade 5-6
MATH WORKBOOK
Step by Step Guide
and Essential Practice
with Answers
Multiplication Division
Place Value and Expanded Notations
Fractions and Geometry
Units and Statistics
MathFlare Publishing

MathFlare
Grade 6
MATH WORKBOOK
Step by Step Guide
and Essential Practice
with Answers
Integers and Statistics
Arithmetic and Pre-Algebra
Fractions and Geometry
Ratio and Percentage
MathFlare Publishing

MathFlare
Grade 6-7
MATH WORKBOOK
Step by Step Guide
and Essential Practice
with Answers
Arithmetic and Pre-Algebra
Ratio, Percent Proportion
Geometry
Statistics
MathFlare Publishing

MathFlare
Grade 7
MATH WORKBOOK
Step by Step Guide
and Essential Practice
with Answers
Pre-Algebra
Ratio, Percent Proportion
Geometry
Statistics
MathFlare Publishing

MathFlare
Grade 7-8
MATH WORKBOOK
Step by Step Guide
and Essential Practice
with Answers
Pre-Algebra
Ratio, Percent Proportion
Geometry and Cartesian Plane
Statistics
MathFlare Publishing

MathFlare
Grade 8-9
MATH WORKBOOK
Step by Step Guide
and Essential Practice
with Answers
Pre-Algebra
Ratio, Proportion and Percentage
Linear Equations
Geometry and Cartesian Plane
MathFlare Publishing

MathFlare
Grade 8
MATH WORKBOOK
Step by Step Guide
and Essential Practice
with Answers
Pre-Algebra
Percentage
Linear Equations
Geometry
MathFlare Publishing

Chapter. 01

Multiplication and Division

Multiplication

Multiplication is an easy way of adding numbers together quickly. Instead of adding the same number repeatedly, we use multiplication to find the total much faster.

For instance, rather than adding 2 + 2 + 2 + 2 + 2, we can multiply 2 by 5 to get the same result: 2 x 5 = 10.

Here, the first number (2) is called the multiplicand, second number (5) is the multiplier. The answer we get, in this case, 10, is called the product.

Let's think of multiplication as repeated addition.

Take 2 x 5, for example. It means adding 2 together five times, which we can illustrate as: 2 + 2 + 2 + 2 + 2 = 10

Multiplication can also be visualized as groups of objects. Imagine we have 2 groups, each containing 5 oranges.

To find the total number of oranges, we multiply the number of groups (2) by the number of oranges in each group (5):

2 groups of 5 oranges = 10 oranges

Expressed as multiplication: 2 x 5 = 10

In summary, multiplication offers various ways to approach it: through repeated addition or by envisioning groups of objects. It's a powerful tool that makes solving math problems much quicker and more efficient!

We can also use the following table to quickly remember multiplication facts. The intersection of two points shows the product of two numbers.

For instance, the product of 5 x 6 = 30, or 6 x 5 = 30.

	1	2	3	4	5	6	7	8	9	10
1	1	2	3	4	5	6	7	8	9	10
2	2	4	6	8	10	12	14	16	18	20
3	3	6	9	12	15	18	21	24	27	30
4	4	8	12	16	20	24	28	32	36	40
5	5	10	15	20	25	30	35	40	45	50
6	6	12	18	24	30	36	42	48	54	60
7	7	14	21	28	35	42	49	56	63	70
8	8	16	24	32	40	48	56	64	72	80
9	9	18	27	36	45	54	63	72	81	90
10	10	20	30	40	50	60	70	80	90	100

Multiplication: 3 x 3

Let's solve problems from exercises:

$$
\begin{array}{r}
422 \\
\times\ 777 \\
\hline
+\quad 2954 \\
+\quad 2954 \\
+\ \underline{2954} \\
=\ 327894
\end{array}
$$

Multi Digit Multiplication

$$
\begin{array}{r}
38{,}518 \\
\times\quad 295 \\
\hline
+\ \ 192590 \\
+346662 \\
+\underline{77036} \\
=1362810
\end{array}
$$

Long Division and Remainders

Division is like the opposite of multiplication. It's all about sharing or distributing items equally among a certain number of groups or people.

When we divide one number by another, we're essentially splitting a number into equal parts. We're figuring out how many groups of a certain size can be made from that number.

For instance, let's divide 20 by 4.

When we divide 20 by 4, we're essentially asking, "How many groups of size 4 can we make from 20?"

Now, there are several parts or terms involved in the division process:

- **Dividend:** This is the number being divided, which in this case, is 20.

- **Divisor:** This is the number we're dividing by, which is 4.

- **Quotient:** This is the answer we get after dividing. It tells us how many groups of divisors can be made from the dividend. In this case, the answer is 5.

- **Remainder:** when the divisor doesn't evenly divide the dividend, we get the remainder.

So, when we divide 20 by 4, we found out that 5 groups of 4 can be made from 20.

Let's solve problems from exercises:

$$
\begin{array}{r}
4 \\
4\overline{)16} \\
-16 \\
\hline
0
\end{array}
\qquad
\begin{array}{r}
42 \\
12\overline{)504} \\
-48 \\
\hline
24 \\
-24 \\
\hline
0
\end{array}
\qquad
\begin{array}{r}
477 \\
6\overline{)2{,}862} \\
-24 \\
\hline
46 \\
-42 \\
\hline
42 \\
-42 \\
\hline
0
\end{array}
\qquad
\begin{array}{r}
8{,}965 \text{ R1} \\
9\overline{)80{,}686} \\
-72 \\
\hline
86 \\
-81 \\
\hline
58 \\
-54 \\
\hline
46 \\
-45 \\
\hline
1
\end{array}
$$

Multiplying Decimals

Multiplying decimals is a lot like multiplying whole numbers, but we need to be careful about where we put the decimal point in the answer.

Step 1: Start by multiplying the numbers together, just like we do with whole numbers. Ignore the decimals for now.

Step 2: Count how many decimal places there are in the numbers we're multiplying. This will tell us how many decimal places our answer should have.

Step 3: Put the decimal point in the answer by starting from the right side of the number. Move the decimal point to the left as many places as there are in the total number of decimal places.

For example, let's multiply 4.5 by 2.5:

Step 1: Multiply the numbers as if they were whole numbers:

$$25 \times 45 = 1125.$$

Step 2: There is one decimal place in 2.5 and one in 4.5, making a total of two decimal places.

Step 3: Starting from the right side of the answer, count two places to the left and put the decimal point there.

So, the final answer is 11.25.

Remember to pay close attention to where the decimal point goes in the answer.

Let's solve a problem:

```
       22.93
   ×    4.69
   ─────────
   +  20637
   + 13758
   +  9172
   ─────────
   =1075417
```

Rewrite the product with
4 decimal places.
So the answer is 107.5417

<u>Dividing Decimals</u>

Dividing decimals is a lot like dividing whole numbers, but we need to be careful about placement of decimal point in the answer.

Steps to follow:

1. **Set up the division problem:** Write the dividend (the number being divided) and the divisor (the number you're dividing by) as you would in a long division problem.

$$1.7\overline{)1.6}$$

2. **Move the decimal:** Move the decimal point to the right in the dividend and divisor by the same number of places.

$$17\overline{)16}$$

3. **Perform the division:** Divide as you would with whole numbers.

$$
\begin{array}{r}
0\,0.9\,4 \\
17\overline{)16} \\
-0 \\
\hline
16 \\
-0 \\
\hline
160 \\
-153 \\
\hline
70 \\
-68 \\
\hline
2
\end{array}
$$

4. **Place the decimal point:** Place the decimal point in the quotient directly above its position in the dividend.

So, the quotient is 0.94.

Using the Power of 10

Using the powers of 10, 100, and 1000 makes multiplying and dividing by these numbers very convenient. Let's illustrate with examples:

Multiplying by Powers of 10:

- To multiply a number by 10, simply move the decimal point one place to the right.

$$5 \times 10 = 50$$

- To multiply a number by 100, move the decimal point two places to the right.

$$5 \times 100 = 500$$

- To multiply a number by 1000, move the decimal point three places to the right.

$$5 \times 1000 = 5000.$$

Dividing by Powers of 10:

- To divide a number by 10, simply move the decimal point one place to the left.

$$50 \div 10 = 5$$

- To divide a number by 100, move the decimal point two places to the left.

$$500 \div 100 = 5$$

- To divide a number by 1000, move the decimal point three places to the left.

$$5000 \div 1000 = 5$$

Using the powers of 10, 100, and 1000 makes multiplying and dividing by these numbers simple and straightforward.

Multiplication and Division Word Problems

Anthony can run four laps in 1 hour. How many laps can Anthony run in 18 hours?

```
       4        1 hour 4 laps
    × 1 8       how many laps can he  run in 18 hours?
    + 3 2
    + 4
    = 7 2      Anthony can run 72 laps in 18 hours
```

How many 12 cm pieces of rope can you cut from a rope that is 420 cm long?

$$
\begin{array}{r}
35 \\
12\overline{)520} \\
-36 \\
\hline
60 \\
-60 \\
\hline
0
\end{array}
$$

35 pieces can be cut

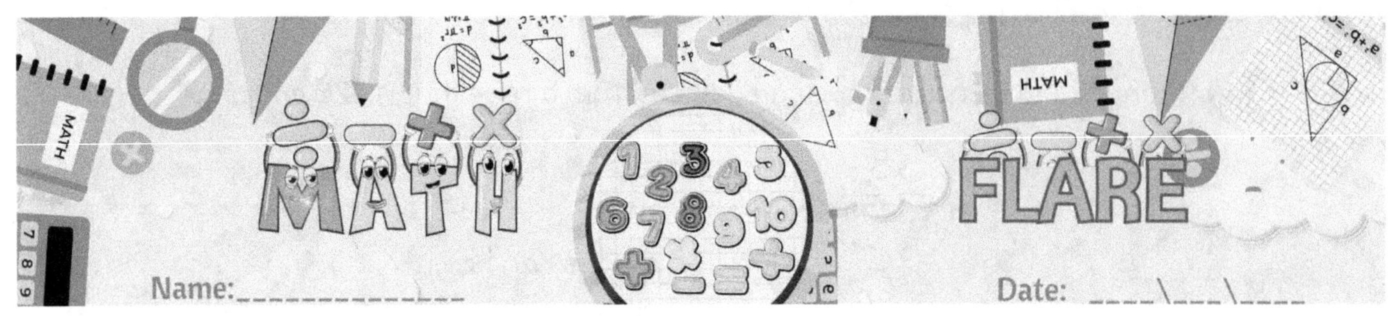

Multiplication: (3 x 3)

Find the product.

1) 422
× 777
+ 2954
+ 2954
+ 2954
= 327894

2) 883
× 389

3) 916
× 305

4) 624
× 953

5) 244
× 889

6) 889
× 104

7) 176
× 192

8) 847
× 732

9) 436
× 557

10) 257
× 563

11) 529
× 700

12) 997
× 428

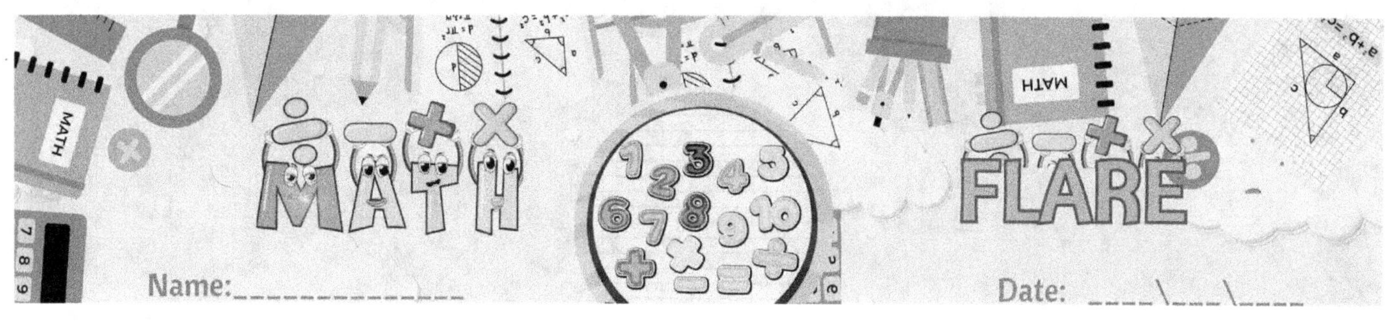

13) 820
   × 337

14) 704
   × 450

15) 394
   × 988

16) 470
   × 557

17) 600
   × 200

18) 465
   × 718

19) 588
   × 546

20) 545
   × 225

21) 278
   × 334

22) 667
   × 406

23) 819
   × 768

24) 522
   × 626

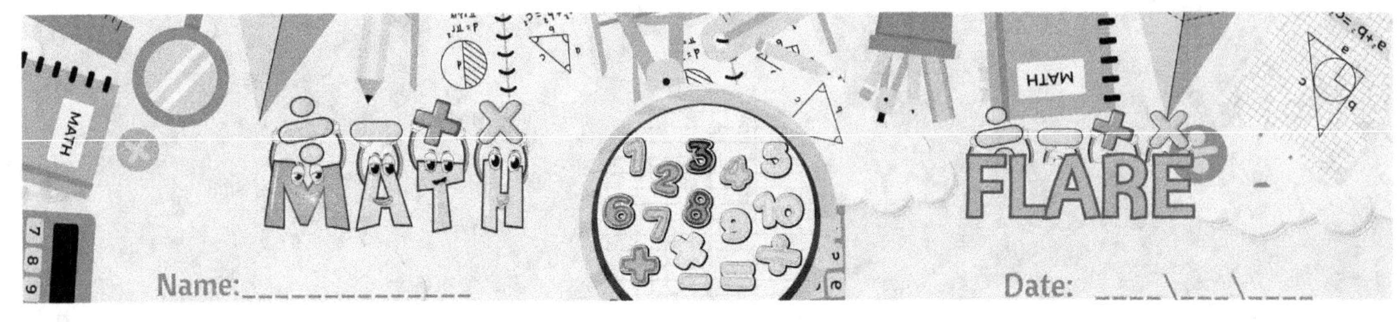

25)   132
    × 365

26)   443
    × 277

27)   991
    × 684

28)   444
    × 720

29)   780
    × 555

30)   568
    × 679

31)   600
    × 274

32)   659
    × 256

33)   519
    × 432

34)   503
    × 974

35)   726
    × 229

36)   112
    × 131

Multi Digit Multiplication

Find the product.

1)   38,518
   ×   295
   + 1 9 2 5 9 0
   + 3 4 6 6 6 2
   + 7 7 0 3 6
   = 1 3 6 2 8 1 0

2)   13,343
   ×   690

3)   60,904
   ×   152

4)   81,444
   ×   178

5)   41,882
   ×   130

6)   64,463
   ×   293

7)   56,584
   ×   915

8)   75,647
   ×   744

9)   93,827
   ×   133

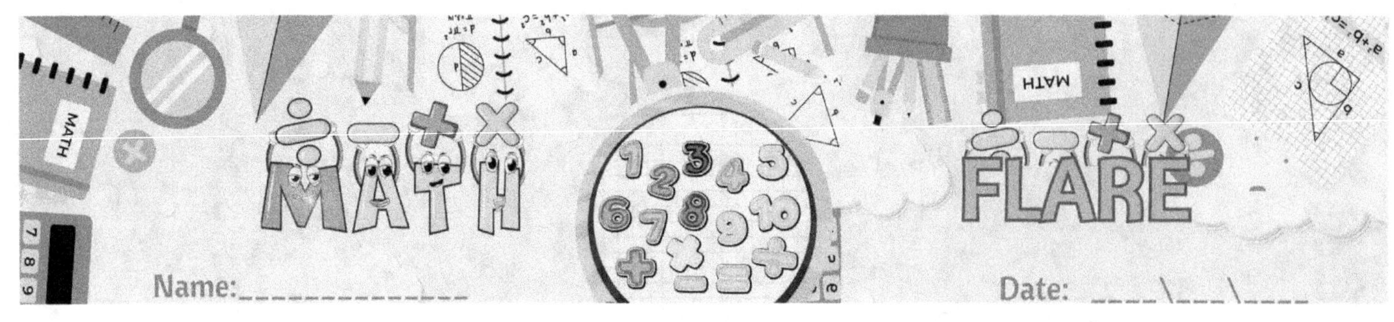

10) 97,847
   ×   865

11) 62,505
   ×   105

12) 67,523
   ×   512

13) 88,699
   ×   487

14) 36,484
   ×   547

15) 90,005
   ×   902

16) 22,035
   ×   554

17) 26,495
   ×   959

18) 39,919
   ×   249

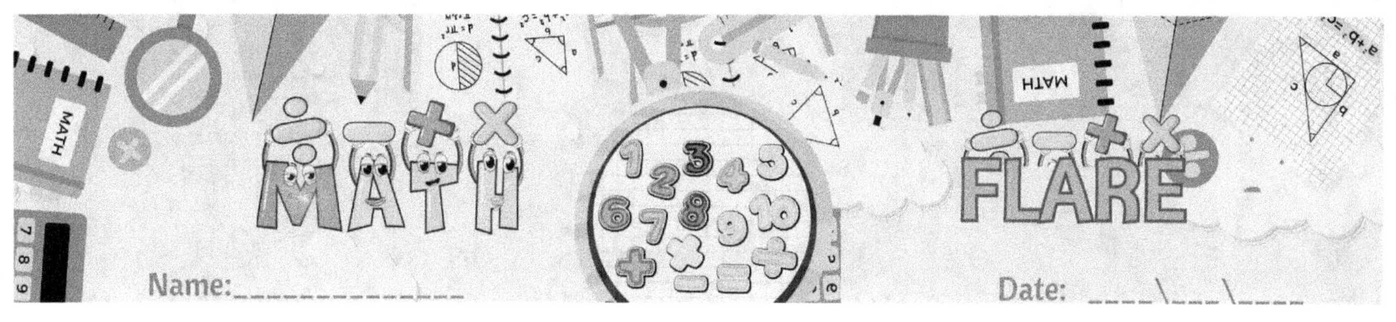

19)   68,742
   ×   189

20)   94,629
   ×   516

21)   86,497
   ×   522

22)   85,484
   ×   629

23)   61,093
   ×   326

24)   86,590
   ×   587

25)   31,884
   ×   980

26)   29,044
   ×   211

27)   91,086
   ×   246

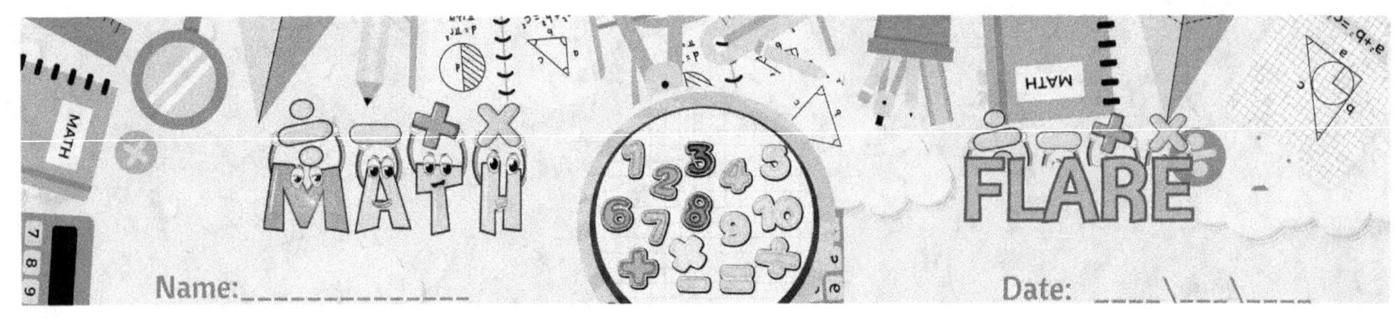

28)   50,636
    ×   380

29)   61,986
    ×   621

30)   80,365
    ×   221

31)   78,688
    ×   367

32)   27,831
    ×   516

33)   90,926
    ×   190

34)   12,818
    ×   605

35)   61,683
    ×   607

36)   15,749
    ×   848

Long Division

Find the quotient.

1)
$$9\,\overline{)\,80{,}686}$$
8,965 R1
- 72
86
- 81
58
- 54
46
- 45
1

2)
$$3\,\overline{)\,51{,}228}$$

3)
$$2\,\overline{)\,93{,}995}$$

4)
$$6\,\overline{)\,48{,}602}$$

5)
$$6\,\overline{)\,29{,}824}$$

6)
$$3\,\overline{)\,52{,}647}$$

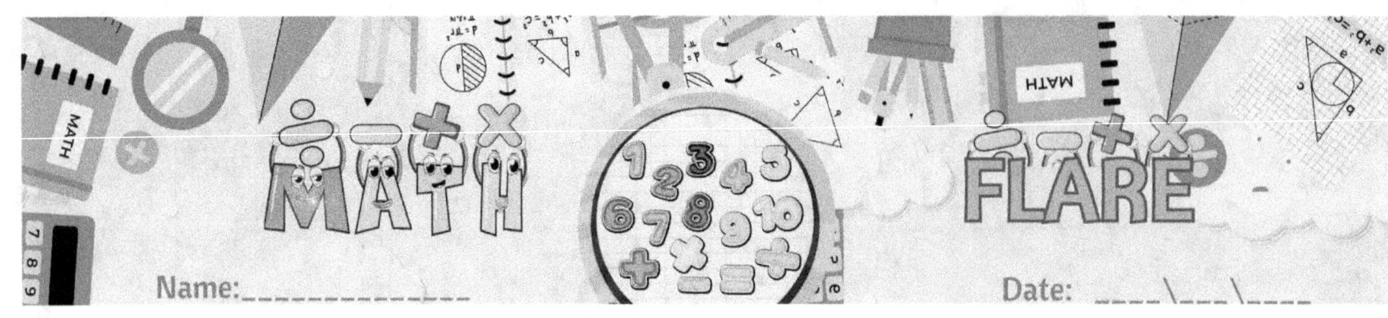

7)

$$6\overline{)20{,}016}$$

8)

$$3\overline{)67{,}706}$$

9)

$$8\overline{)81{,}904}$$

10)

$$3\overline{)26{,}813}$$

11)

$$2\overline{)34{,}767}$$

12)

$$8\overline{)50{,}465}$$

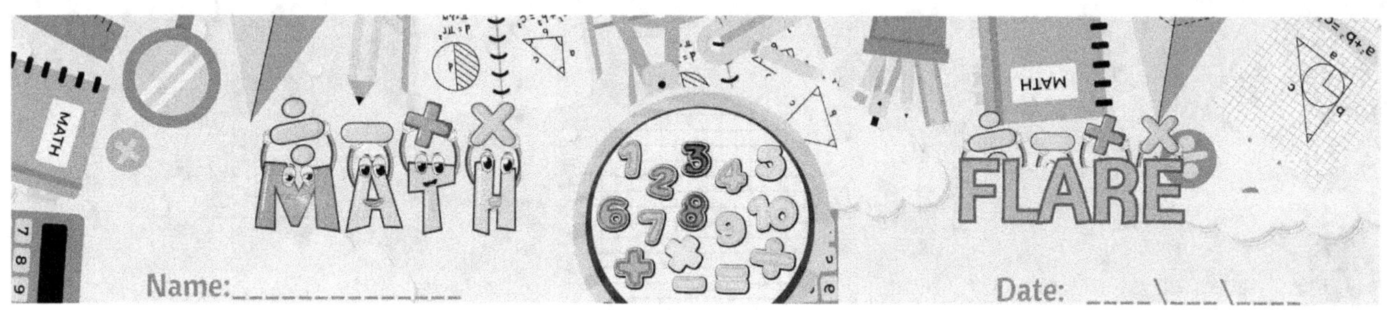

13)

6 ⟌ 11,294

14)

3 ⟌ 73,953

15)

2 ⟌ 63,575

16)

9 ⟌ 38,813

17)

9 ⟌ 43,504

18)

6 ⟌ 46,777

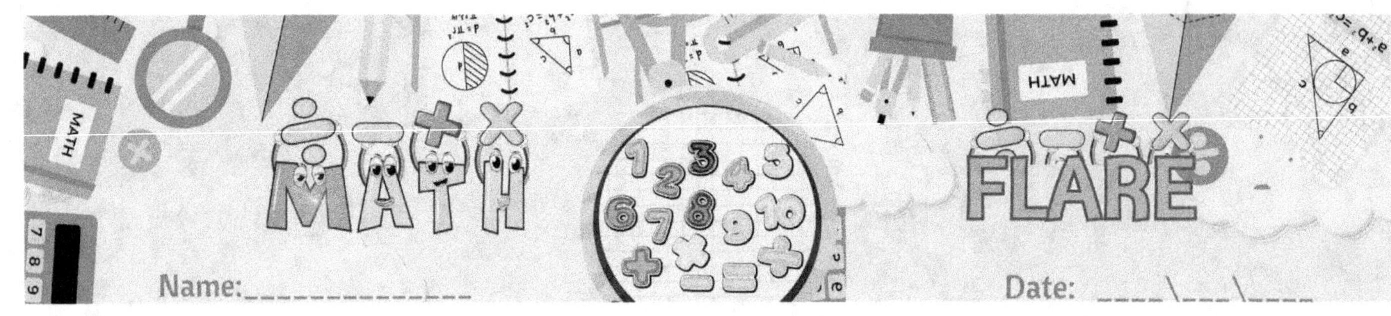

19)

$$4\overline{)62{,}595}$$

20)

$$4\overline{)42{,}379}$$

21)

$$4\overline{)46{,}792}$$

22)

$$9\overline{)44{,}813}$$

23)

$$10\overline{)99{,}046}$$

24)

$$7\overline{)20{,}822}$$

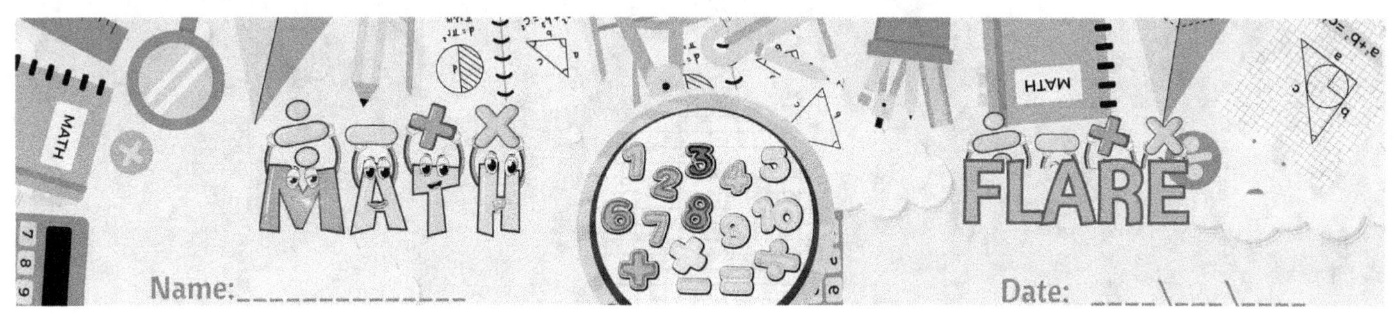

25)

10) 46,749

26)

2) 80,039

27)

6) 67,792

28)

8) 42,895

29)

8) 48,857

30)

6) 15,728

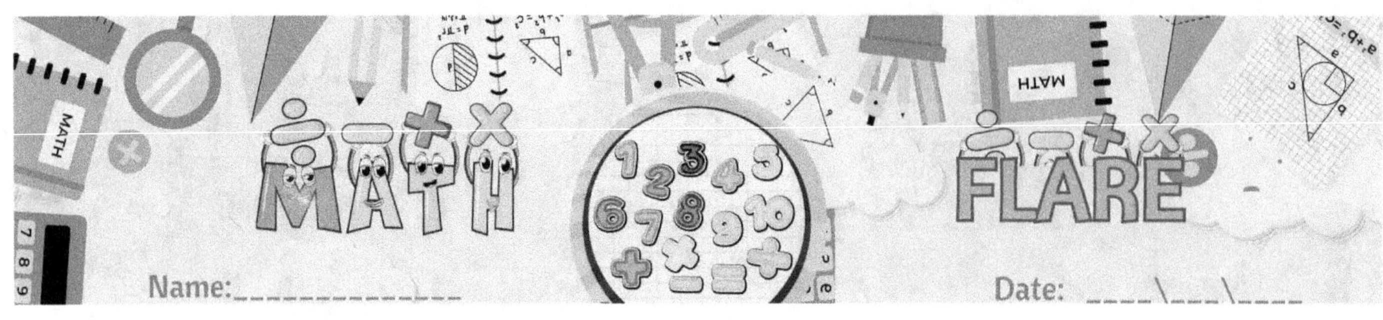

31)

5 ⟌ 40,765

32)

3 ⟌ 90,205

33)

6 ⟌ 27,022

34)

4 ⟌ 77,175

35)

3 ⟌ 13,206

36)

6 ⟌ 63,087

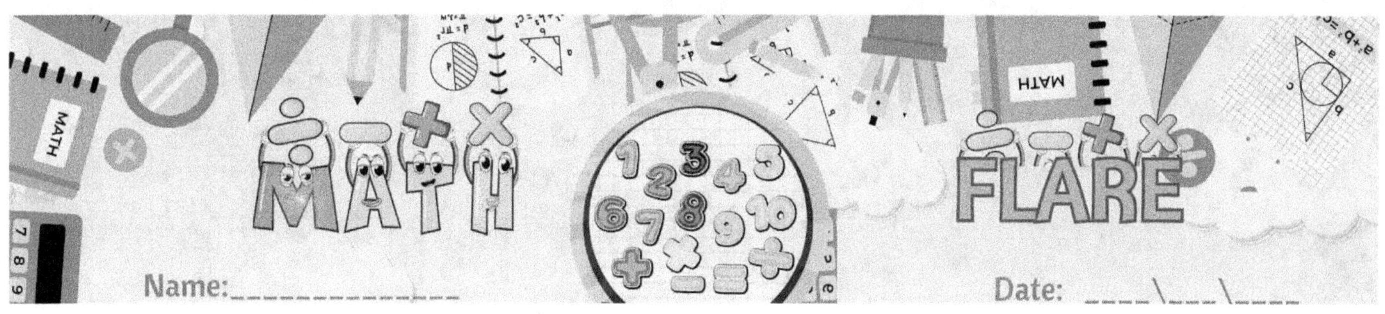

37)

9)‾43,054

38)

10)‾73,706

39)

6)‾70,211

40)

3)‾74,867

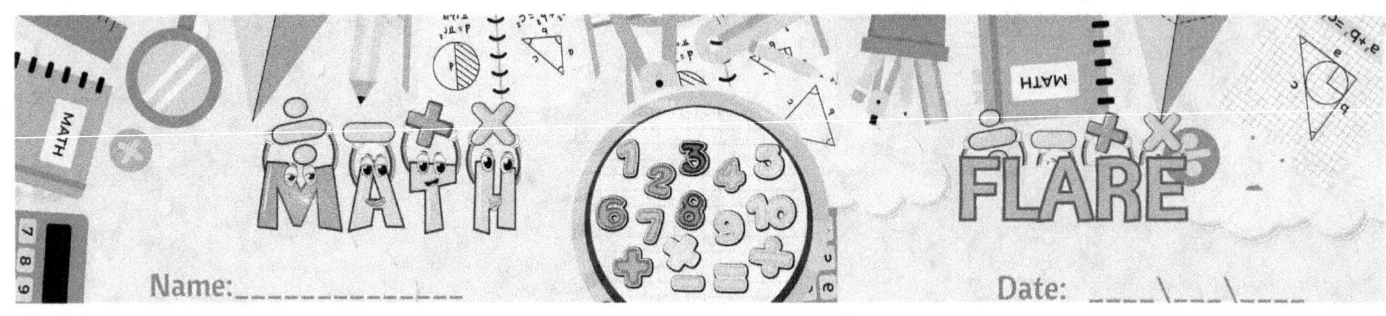

Long Division: Remainders

Find the quotient.

1)
$$18\overline{)59{,}637}$$ 3,313 R3

$$
\begin{array}{r}
-54 \\ \hline
56 \\
-54 \\ \hline
23 \\
-18 \\ \hline
57 \\
-54 \\ \hline
3
\end{array}
$$

2)
$$13\overline{)33{,}457}$$

3)
$$6\overline{)79{,}463}$$

4)
$$5\overline{)29{,}680}$$

5)

$$6 \overline{)\,32{,}160}$$

6)

$$12 \overline{)\,49{,}589}$$

7)

$$17 \overline{)\,67{,}298}$$

8)

$$7 \overline{)\,90{,}561}$$

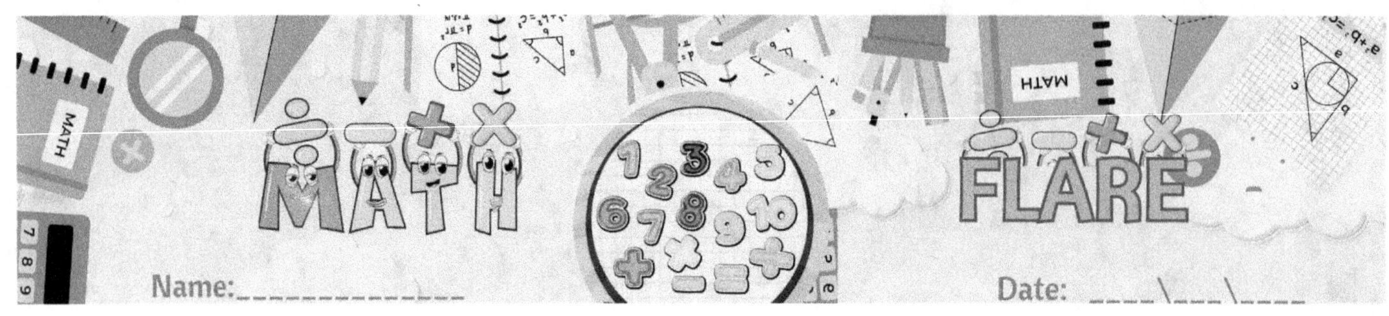

Name:_________________   Date: _______________

9)

$$15\overline{)95{,}751}$$

10)

$$9\overline{)98{,}329}$$

11)

$$4\overline{)78{,}518}$$

12)

$$6\overline{)90{,}281}$$

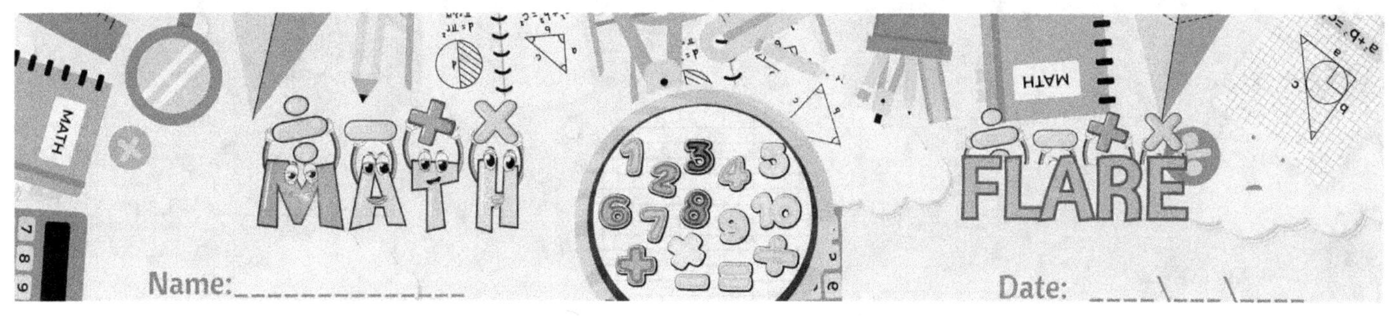

13)

14) 36,120

14)

11) 69,051

15)

13) 83,228

16)

10) 91,785

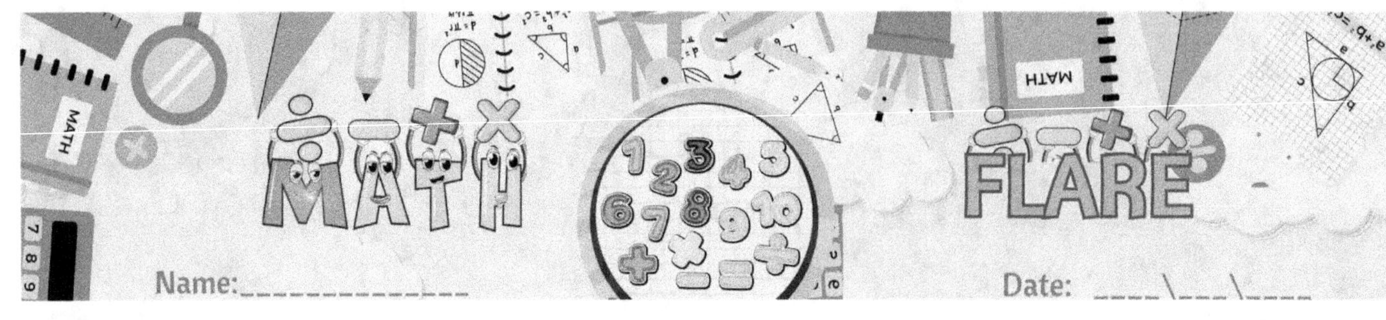

17)

$$2 \overline{)50{,}055}$$

18)

$$8 \overline{)11{,}828}$$

19)

$$3 \overline{)69{,}280}$$

20)

$$10 \overline{)91{,}867}$$

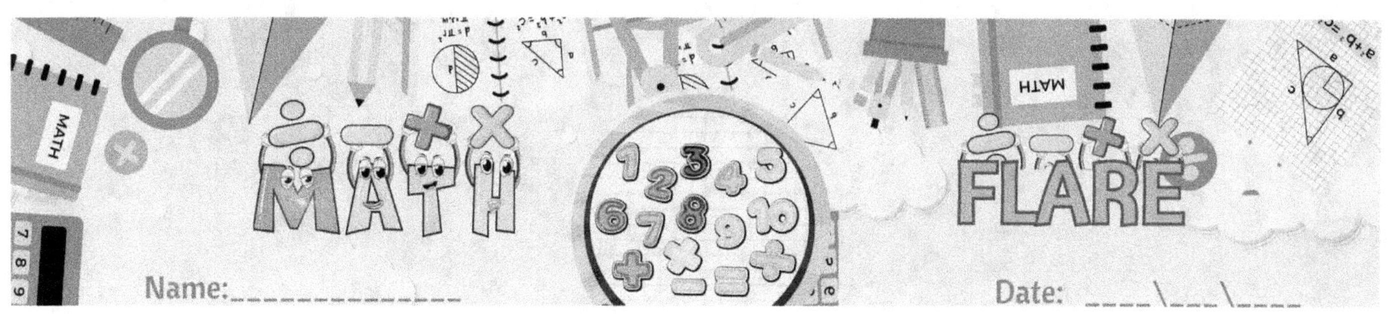

21)

$10 \overline{)16{,}617}$

22)

$19 \overline{)54{,}584}$

23)

$8 \overline{)40{,}902}$

24)

$4 \overline{)82{,}806}$

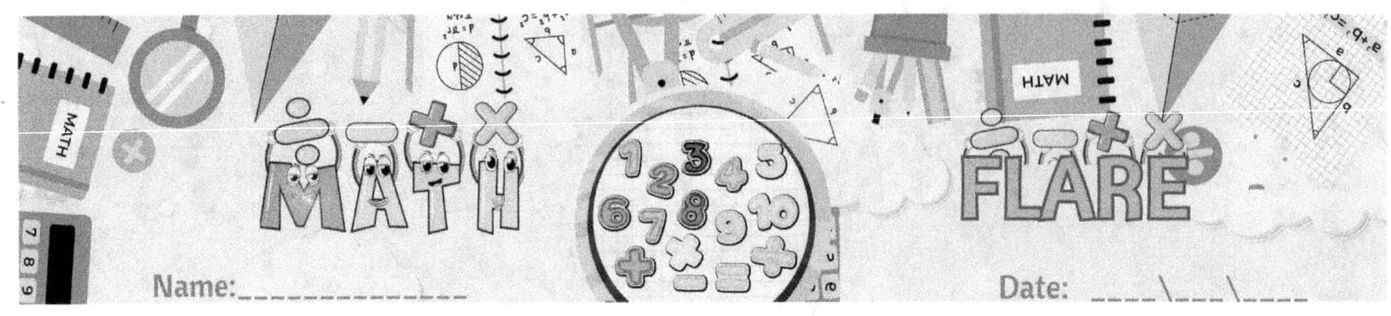

25)

$$17 \overline{\smash{)}87{,}767}$$

26)

$$5 \overline{\smash{)}94{,}213}$$

27)

$$12 \overline{\smash{)}99{,}589}$$

28)

$$10 \overline{\smash{)}54{,}813}$$

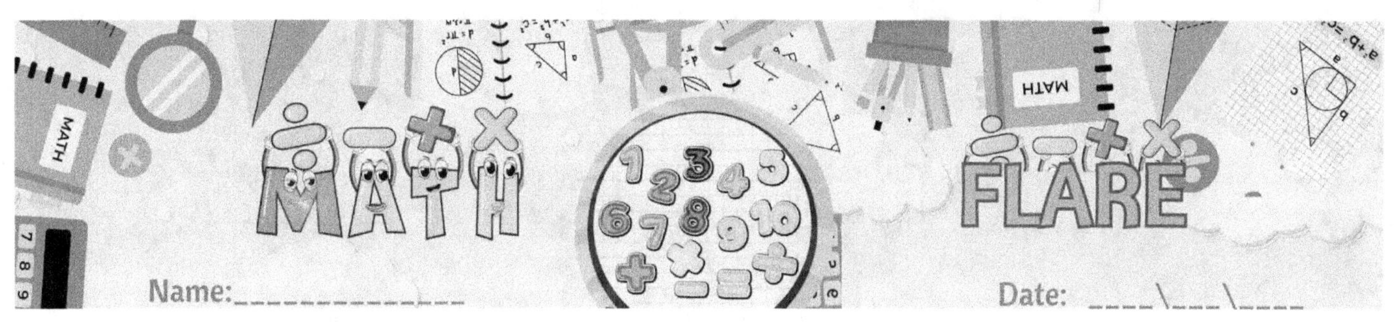

Multiplying Decimals
Find the product.

1)
$$\begin{array}{r} 98.72 \\ \times\ \ 1.23 \\ \hline 29616 \\ 19744\ \ \\ 9872\ \ \ \ \\ \hline 121.4256 \end{array}$$

2)
$$\begin{array}{r} 40.62 \\ \times\ \ 2.17 \\ \hline \end{array}$$

3)
$$\begin{array}{r} 60.87 \\ \times\ \ 7.35 \\ \hline \end{array}$$

4)
$$\begin{array}{r} 42.17 \\ \times\ \ 6.81 \\ \hline \end{array}$$

5)
$$\begin{array}{r} 39.24 \\ \times\ \ 9.79 \\ \hline \end{array}$$

6)
$$\begin{array}{r} 21.77 \\ \times\ \ 6.62 \\ \hline \end{array}$$

7)
$$\begin{array}{r} 82.33 \\ \times\ \ 6.24 \\ \hline \end{array}$$

8)
$$\begin{array}{r} 68.11 \\ \times\ \ 9.20 \\ \hline \end{array}$$

9)
$$\begin{array}{r} 81.41 \\ \times\ \ 5.81 \\ \hline \end{array}$$

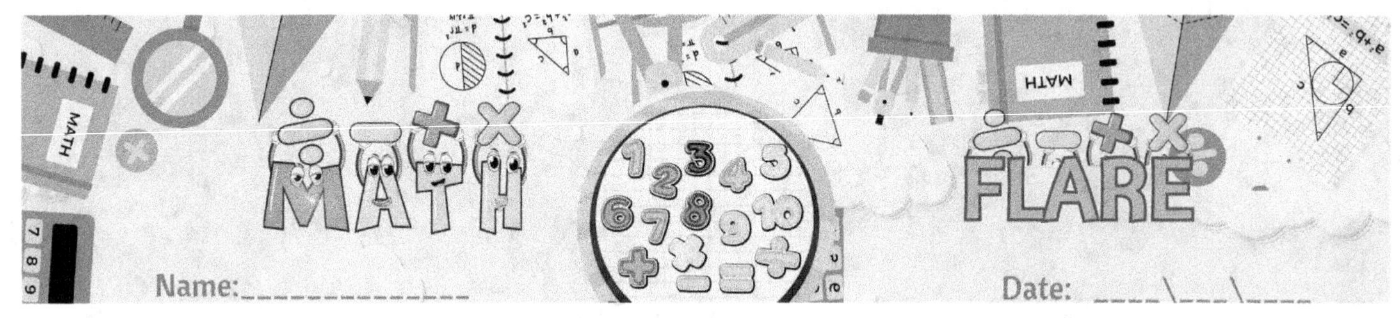

10)   39.08
    × 3.83
    ____

11)   64.18
    × 9.34
    ____

12)   90.22
    × 9.82
    ____

13)   84.89
    × 6.01
    ____

14)   68.37
    × 9.63
    ____

15)   69.82
    × 7.91
    ____

16)   51.95
    × 8.79
    ____

17)   56.18
    × 6.09
    ____

18)   39.34
    × 6.69
    ____

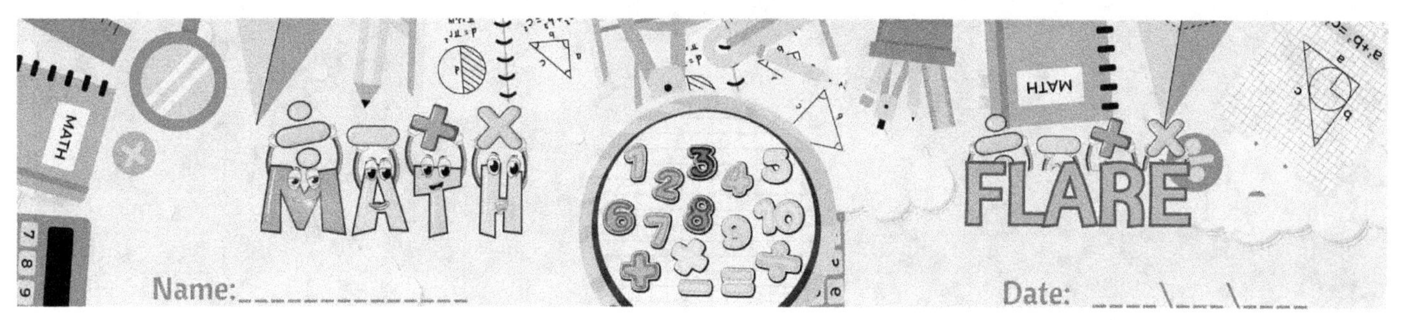

19)   73.08
    ×   8.00

20)   89.28
    ×   4.30

21)   17.99
    ×   8.64

22)   67.51
    ×   4.28

23)   26.09
    ×   2.65

24)   36.52
    ×   3.53

25)   28.75
    ×   1.22

26)   41.21
    ×   5.14

27)   32.96
    ×   2.64

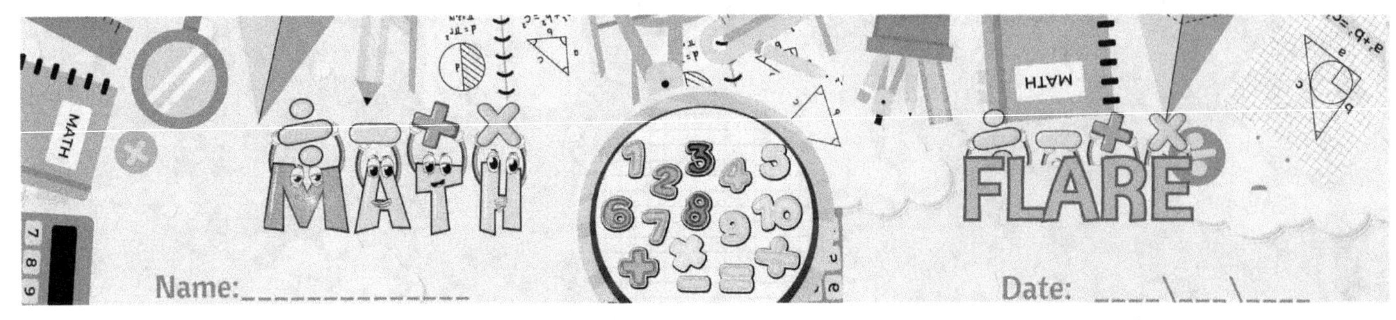

28)   86.68
   ×   1.52

29)   22.10
   ×   4.23

30)   36.85
   ×   1.07

31)   15.16
   ×   4.58

32)   98.28
   ×   6.00

33)   56.07
   ×   3.37

34)   20.11
   ×   3.14

35)   33.14
   ×   1.12

36)   28.96
   ×   1.13

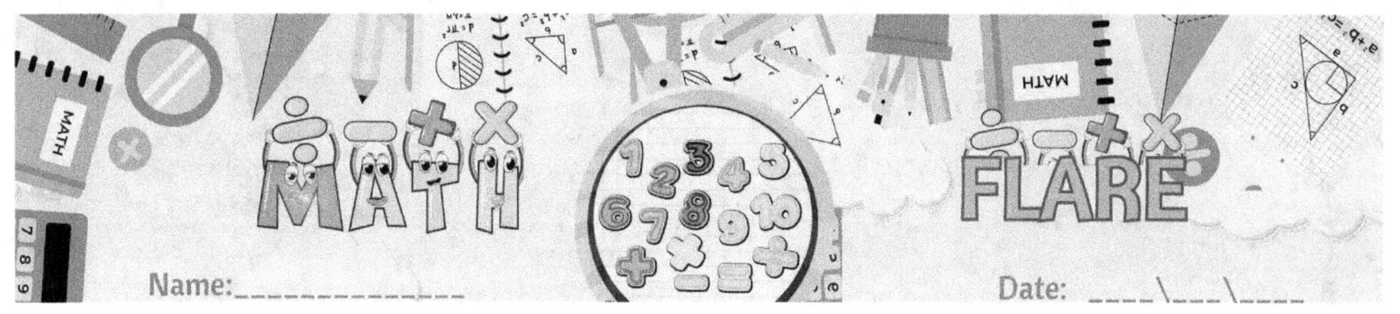

37) 68.87
  × 9.59

38) 30.36
  × 7.76

39) 36.00
  × 5.73

40) 82.16
  × 6.83

41) 33.67
  × 4.31

42) 77.60
  × 6.76

43) 47.95
  × 1.05

44) 65.04
  × 3.97

45) 74.27
  × 3.41

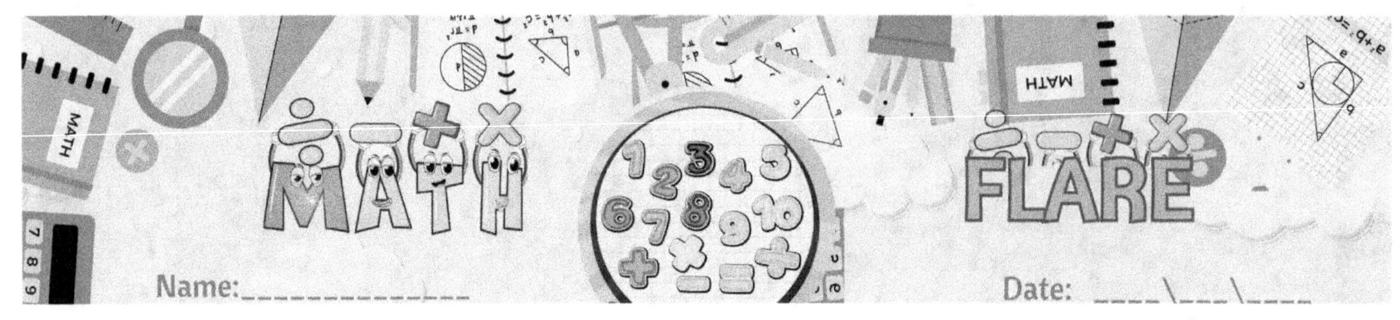

46) 54.85
   × 4.07

47) 53.26
   × 8.85

48) 37.92
   × 7.21

49) 88.17
   × 1.74

50) 86.78
   × 9.22

51) 16.40
   × 1.51

52) 12.14
   × 2.76

53) 83.20
   × 3.99

54) 82.54
   × 3.69

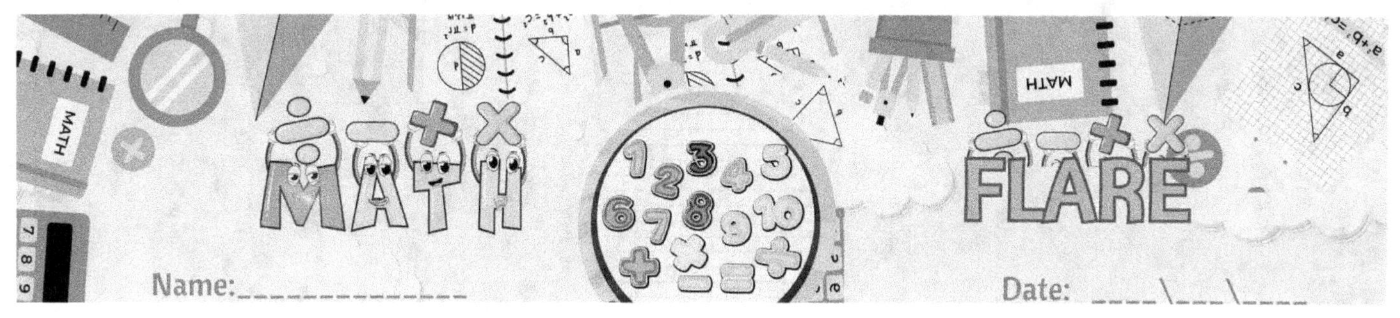

55)
$$\begin{array}{r} 96.08 \\ \times\ \ 1.90 \\ \hline \end{array}$$

56)
$$\begin{array}{r} 79.19 \\ \times\ \ 6.47 \\ \hline \end{array}$$

57)
$$\begin{array}{r} 60.20 \\ \times\ \ 6.84 \\ \hline \end{array}$$

58)
$$\begin{array}{r} 77.00 \\ \times\ \ 7.20 \\ \hline \end{array}$$

59)
$$\begin{array}{r} 68.20 \\ \times\ \ 4.06 \\ \hline \end{array}$$

60)
$$\begin{array}{r} 22.12 \\ \times\ \ 5.55 \\ \hline \end{array}$$

61)
$$\begin{array}{r} 68.71 \\ \times\ \ 8.03 \\ \hline \end{array}$$

62)
$$\begin{array}{r} 57.10 \\ \times\ \ 9.89 \\ \hline \end{array}$$

63)
$$\begin{array}{r} 56.31 \\ \times\ \ 8.82 \\ \hline \end{array}$$

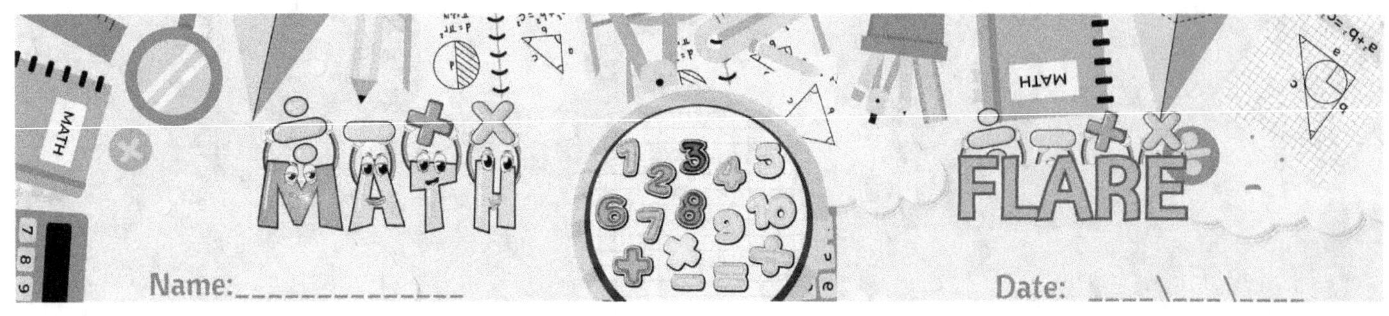

Dividing Decimals
Find the quotient.

1)
$$8\overline{)97.5}$$

```
  12.187
8)97.5
  -8
   17
  -16
    15
    -8
    70
   -64
    60
   -56
     4
```

2)
$$12\overline{)63.2}$$

3)
$$19\overline{)76.7}$$

4)
$$8\overline{)89.1}$$

5)
$$11\overline{)89.6}$$

6)
$$10\overline{)96.8}$$

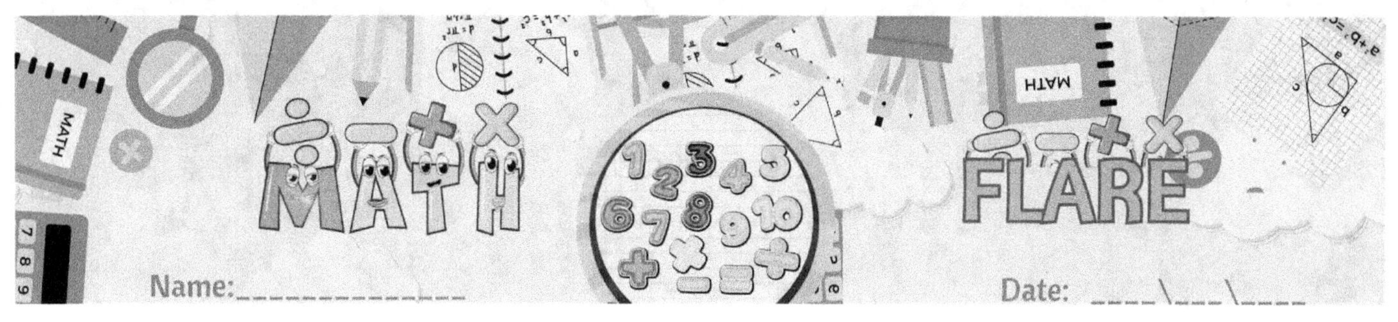

7) $17\overline{)56.6}$

8) $16\overline{)55.6}$

9) $5\overline{)95.9}$

10) $4\overline{)37.3}$

11) $9\overline{)43.1}$

12) $10\overline{)59.2}$

13) $13\overline{)25.8}$

14) $18\overline{)81.7}$

15) $16\overline{)99.0}$

16)

$8 \overline{)72.7}$

17)

$17 \overline{)24.5}$

18)

$16 \overline{)56.4}$

19)

$10 \overline{)13.5}$

20)

$2 \overline{)94.6}$

21)

$5 \overline{)85.9}$

22)

$10 \overline{)11.8}$

23)

$7 \overline{)43.6}$

24)

$15 \overline{)16.2}$

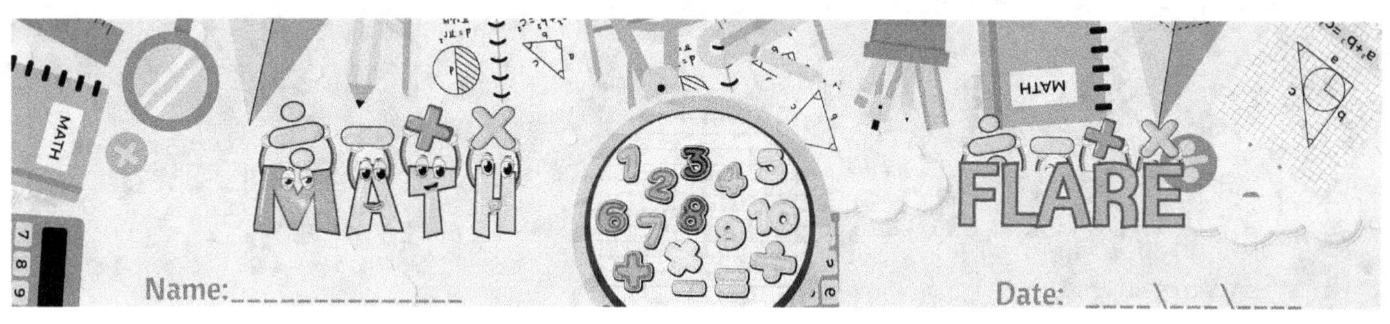

25)

5) 16.9

26)

17) 26.6

27)

16) 78.1

28)

11) 83.4

29)

3) 83.7

30)

3) 44.9

31)

20) 23.5

32)

3) 46.4

33)

12) 82.5

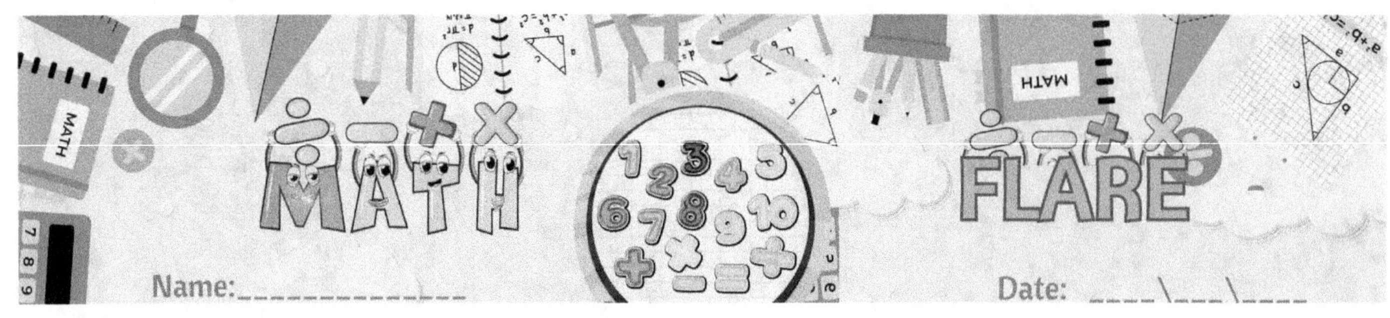

34)

$$14\overline{)37.4}$$

35)

$$15\overline{)39.2}$$

36)

$$11\overline{)78.7}$$

37)

$$5\overline{)36.5}$$

38)

$$4\overline{)40.5}$$

39)

$$3\overline{)47.2}$$

40)

$$17\overline{)17.9}$$

41)

$$2\overline{)59.5}$$

42)

$$16\overline{)82.2}$$

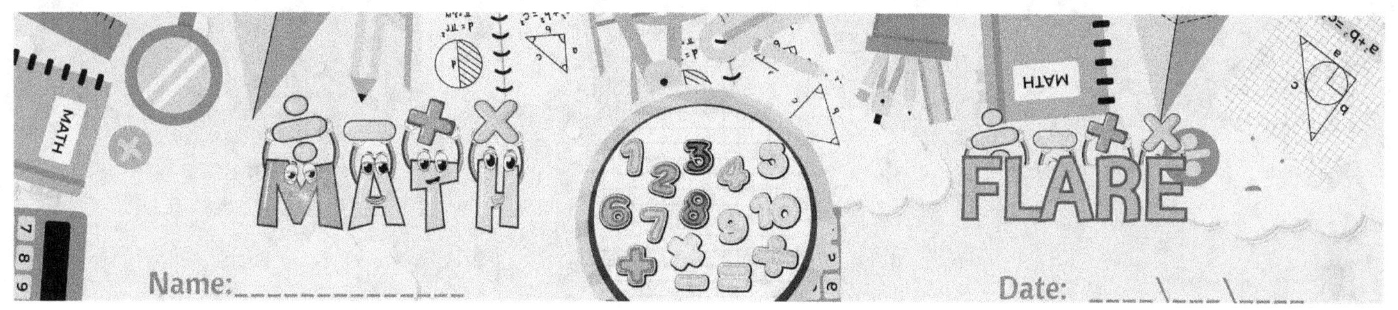

Multiplication Word Problems

1) Kai can run four laps in 1 hour. How many laps can Kai run in 11 hour?

$$
\begin{array}{rl}
4 & \text{4 laps in one hour} \\
\times 11 & \text{how many laps in 11 hours?} \\
+\ 4 & \\
+\ 4 & \\
\hline
= 44 & \text{So, Kai can run 44 laps in 11 hours}
\end{array}
$$

2) A box contains 15 bottles of juice, and each bottle contains six ounces of juice. How many ounces of juice are there in total?

3) Abigail has two vases of flowers. Each vase has 13 flowers. How many flowers does Abigail have in all?

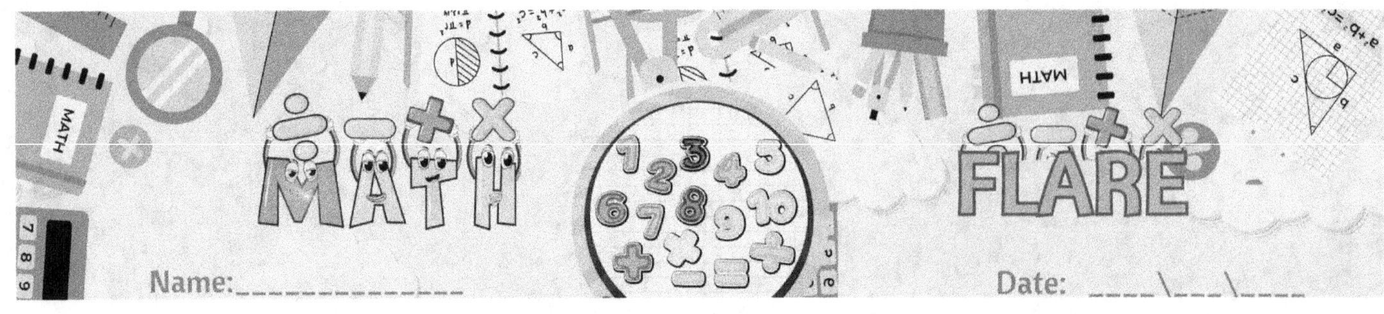

4) If a car travels at three miles per hour for 13 hours, how far will it go?

5) Vincent earns 19 dollars per hour. How much will Vincent earn after working for four hours?

6) Jace can lift four pounds of weight. How many pounds of weight can he lift in 18 repetitions?

7) Jackson can make nine sandwiches in 1 hour. How many sandwiches can he make in 11 hour?

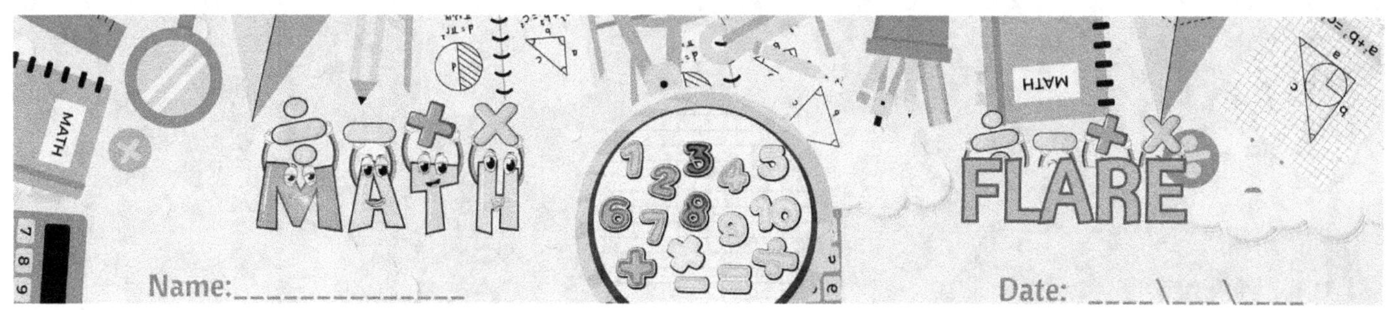

8) There are 11 pants in each bag. If Avery buys 18 bags, how many pants will Avery have?

9) Lillian has 13 yards of fabric, and each dress requires two yards of fabric. How many dresses can Lillian make?

10) There are 12 cars in a parking lot. If each car needs 20 liters of gasoline, how many liters of gasoline are needed for all the cars?

11) A garden has three rows of flowers and 15 flowers in each row. How many flowers are there in total?

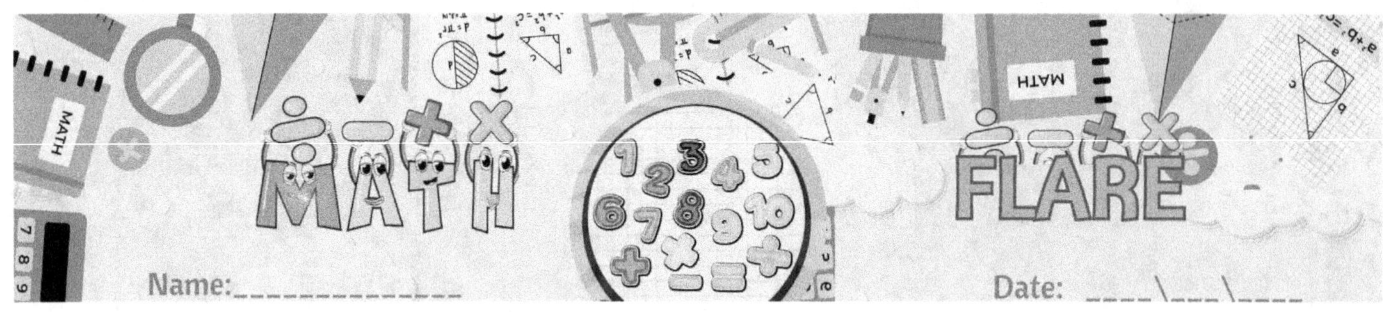

12) Dominic can lift 15 pounds of weight. How many pounds of weight can Dominic lift in total if he lifts for nine sets?

13) Elijah runs six miles every day. How many miles will Elijah run in 15 days?

14) Nolan can solve 17 math problems in one hour. How many problems can Nolan solve in seven hours?

15) Isabelle has 19 books on each shelf, and there are four shelves. How many books does Isabelle have in total?

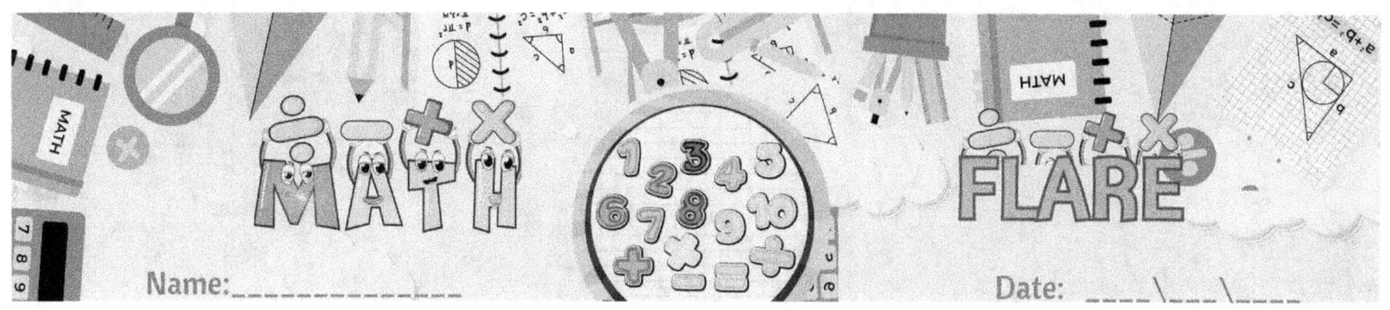

16) Olivia wants to make six pizzas, and each pizza requires 13 cups of cheese. How many cups of cheese does Olivia have?

17) If a boat travels at 17 miles per hour for 11 hours, how far will it go?

18) Amelia wants to make five flower arrangements, and each arrangement requires 16 flowers. How many flowers does Amelia need in total?

19) Paisley has seven jars of jam. Each jar has 16 ounces of jam. How many ounces of jam does Paisley have in all?

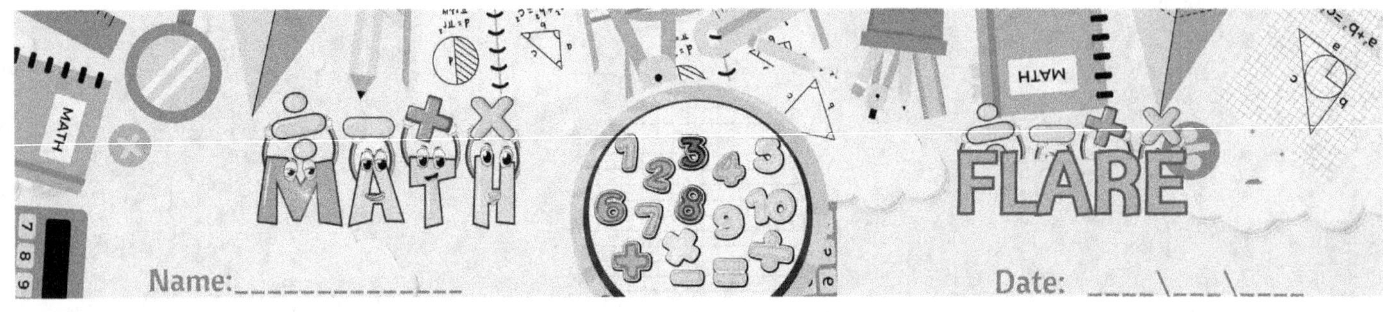

20) There are three shelves in a library. 13 books can fit on each shelf. How many books the library have in total?

21) There are 14 pencils in each pack. If Maria buys 15 packs, how many pencils will Maria have?

22) Hunter sells 17 cakes each day at his bakery. If he works 13 days, how many cakes does he sell?

23) Bella has 13 containers of paint. Each container holds eight liters of paint. How many liters of paint does Bella have in total?

24) Ryder can lift 14 kilograms of weight. How many kilograms of weight can he lift in six lifts?

25) Nathan can do 10 pushups in one minute. How many pushups can Nathan do in 15 minutes?

26) Kennedy has 14 books. Each book has 17 pages. How many pages does Kennedy have in all?

27) Ariana baked 11 batches of cakes. Each batch had six cakes. How many cakes did Ariana bake in all?

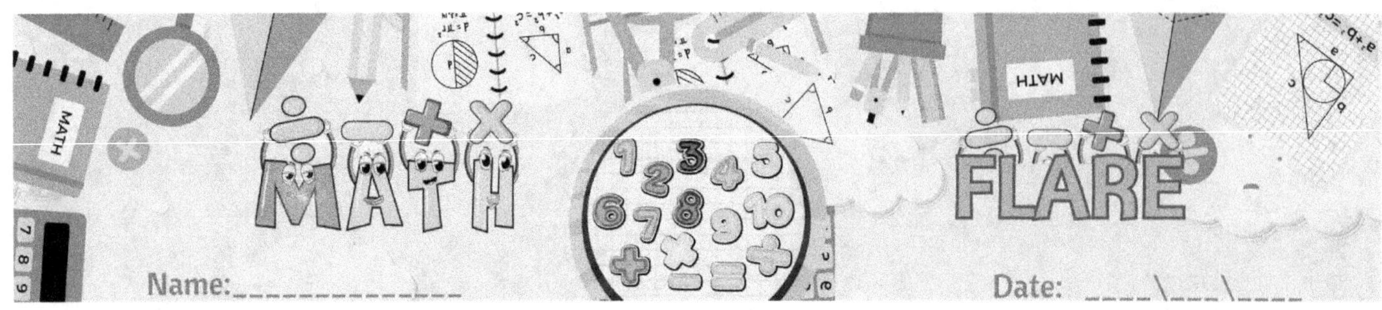

28) If a train travels at five miles per hour for 10 hours, how far will it go?

29) A movie theater can seat 17 people. How many people can it seat in seven showings?

30) There are 20 seats on a bus. If eight buses are needed to transport a group of people, how many people can the group consist of at most?

Division Word Problems

1) Nova has 388 books. If Nova divides them evenly among four children, how many books will each child get?

```
       97
   4 ) 388
      -36
       28        Each child will get 97 books.
      -28
        0
```

2) A book has 110 chapters. If you want to read the book in 10 days, how many chapters do you need to read per day?

3) Madison baked 136 cakes for a party. If she wants to divide them into four equal portions, how many cakes will each portion have?

4) If a box contains 192 Cameras and each person can have four Cameras, how many people can be served from that box?

5) Oliver has 715 dollars and wants to buy 11 oranges. How much can he spend on each oranges?

6) James drove 460 miles in 10 hours. What was James's average speed in miles per hour?

7) If the pizzas have 517 slices and is divided equally among 11 people, how many slices will each person get?

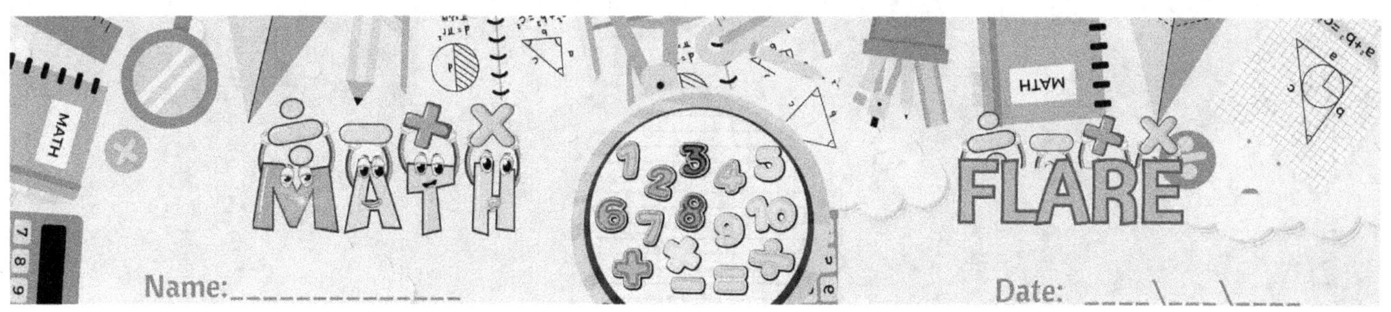

8) A recipe calls for 1,121 cups of sugar to make 19 cookies. How much sugar is needed to make 1 cookie?

9) You have 615 Flashlights and want to share them equally with 15 people. How many Flashlights would each person get?

10) Dylan scored 45 points in nine games. What is his average score per game?

11) A rope is 1,125 meters long. If you cut it into 15 equal pieces, how long is each piece?

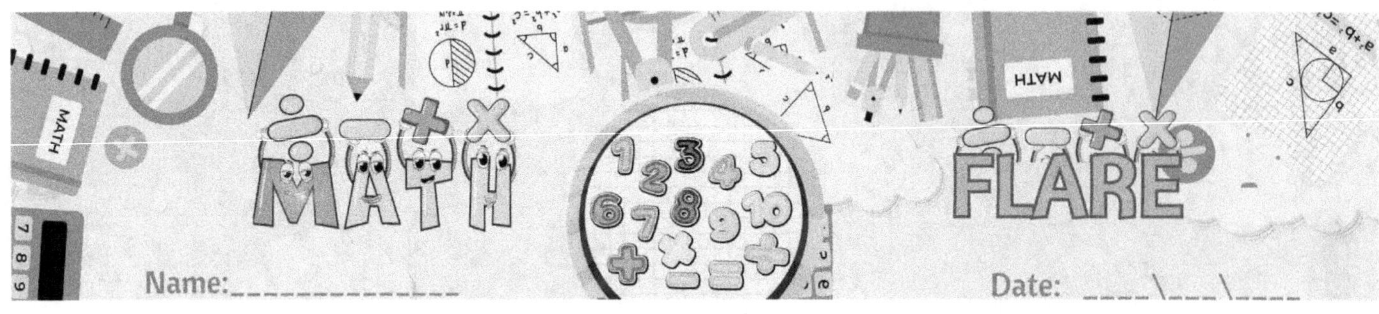

12) Brielle is packing 231 cupcakes into boxes. Each box can hold 11 cupcakes. How many boxes will Brielle need?

13) How many 17 cm pieces of rope can you cut from a rope that is 170 cm long?

14) Emilia bought 17 Diapers for a total of $969. How much did each Diapers cost?

15) Naomi has 420 cookies and wants to divide them equally into seven bags. How many cookies will be in each bag?

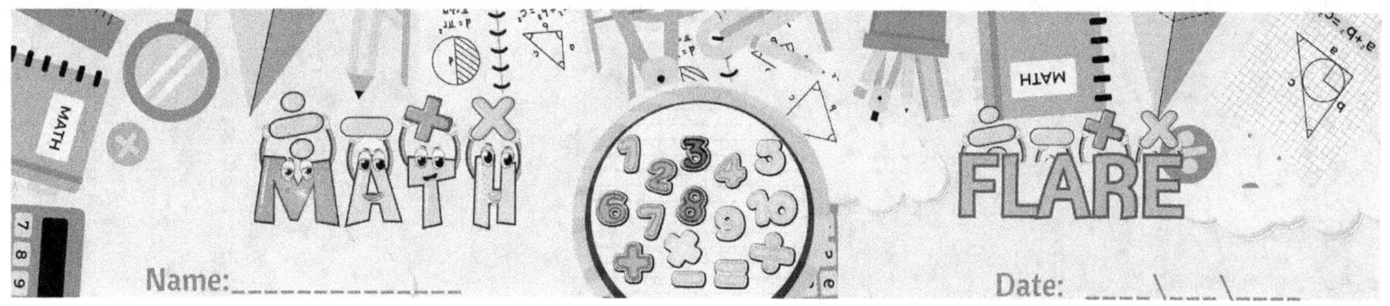

16) If a box contains 504 chocolates and each person can have seven chocolates, how many people can be served from that box?

17) Elijah is reading a book with 240 pages. If Elijah wants to read the same number of pages every day, how many pages would Elijah have to read each day to finish in 20 days?

18) A box of toys weighs 210 pounds. If one toy weighs six pounds, how many toys are there in the box?

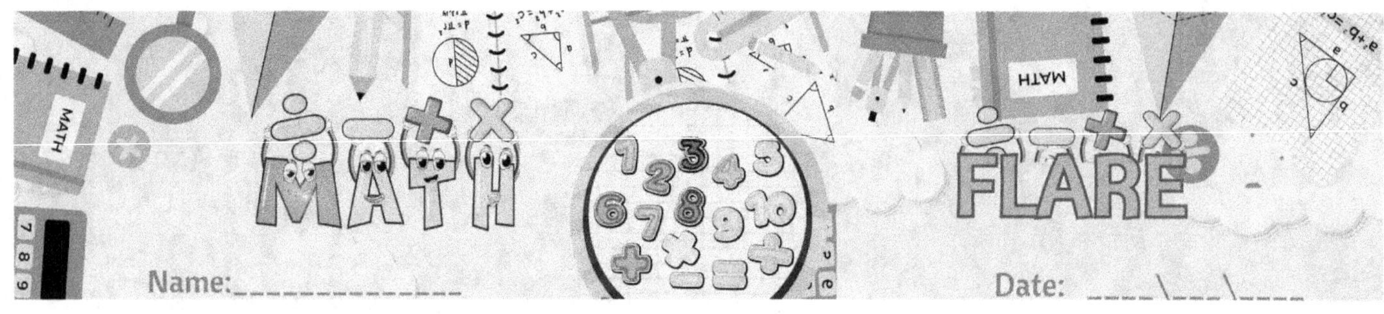

19) If a garden is 368 feet wide and it is divided into eight equal parts, how wide is each part?

20) If Colton has 1,102 Spoons and wants to share them equally among 19 friends, how many Spoons will each friend get?

21) Reagan is filling up water bottles. Each bottle holds 14 ounces of water. If Reagan has 1,316 ounces of water, how many water bottles can she fill up?

22) A box of Balls has 1,710 Balls. If 19 children each get an equal number of Balls, how many Balls will each child get?

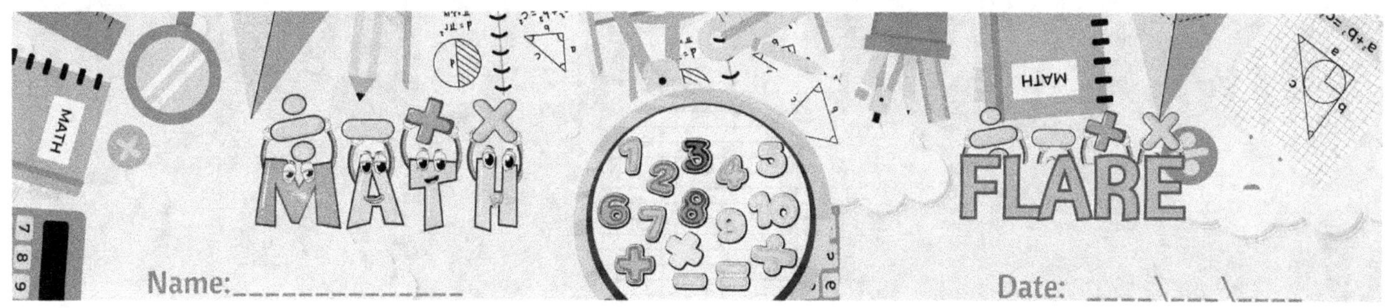

23) Leah has $435 and she wants to buy 15 Jackets that cost the same amount. How much does each Jackets cost?

24) If a garden is 240 feet long and it is divided into 16 equal parts, how long is each part?

25) If Ella has 225 plums and wants to divide them equally among five friends, how many plums will each friend get?

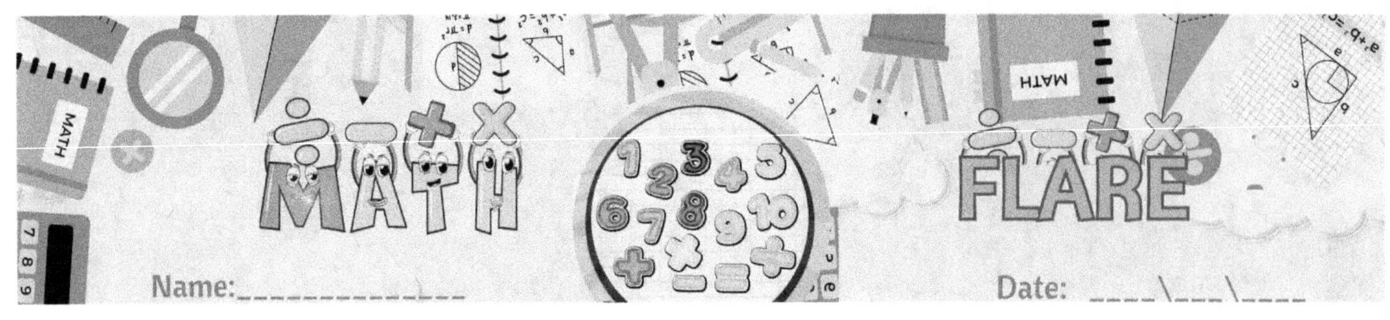

Using the Power of 10

1)
$$100\overline{)90} = 0.9$$

2)
$$\begin{array}{r} 11 \\ \times\ 10 \\ \hline \end{array}$$

3)
$$\begin{array}{r} 67 \\ \times\ 100 \\ \hline \end{array}$$

4)
$$1,000\overline{)57}$$

5)
$$\begin{array}{r} 96 \\ \times\ 1,000 \\ \hline \end{array}$$

6)
$$\begin{array}{r} 73 \\ \times\ 1,000 \\ \hline \end{array}$$

7)
$$\begin{array}{r} 26 \\ \times\ 10 \\ \hline \end{array}$$

8)
$$100\overline{)98}$$

9)
$$100\overline{)70}$$

10)
$$\begin{array}{r} 40 \\ \times\ 100 \\ \hline \end{array}$$

11)
$$\begin{array}{r} 41 \\ \times\ 100 \\ \hline \end{array}$$

12)
$$100\overline{)21}$$

13)
$$\begin{array}{r} 47 \\ \times\ 100 \\ \hline \end{array}$$

14)
$$100\overline{)91}$$

15)
$$\begin{array}{r} 62 \\ \times\ 10 \\ \hline \end{array}$$

16)
$$100\overline{)93}$$

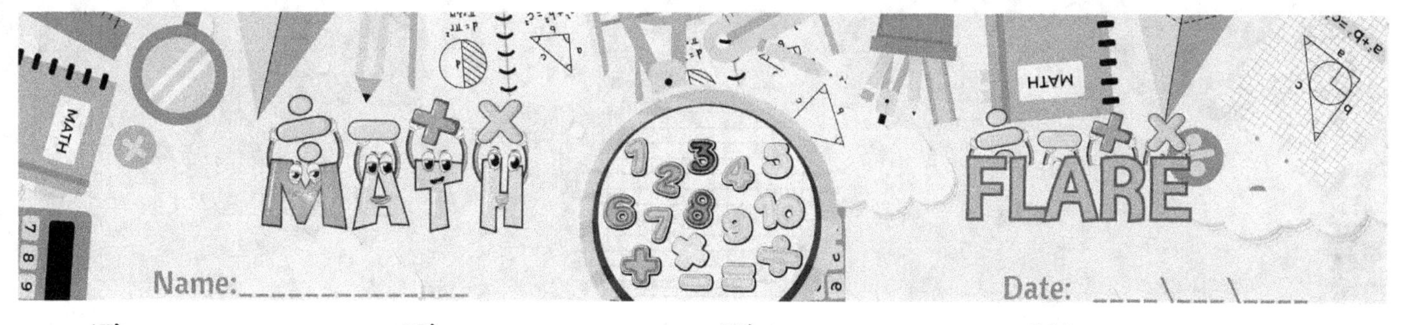

17) 13
× 1,000

18) 52
× 1,000

19) 16
× 1,000

20) 92
× 100

21) 72
× 1,000

22) 10) 81

23) 69
× 100

24) 10) 57

25) 12
× 100

26) 1,000) 12

27) 10) 82

28) 24
× 1,000

29) 29
× 100

30) 100) 95

31) 100) 11

32) 100) 50

33)   76
    × 100

34) 1,000)‾39‾

35) 1,000)‾74‾

36) 100)‾34‾

37) 10)‾34‾

38) 10)‾85‾

39)   53
    × 10

40) 100)‾77‾

41) 100)‾55‾

42)   14
    × 1,000

43) 10)‾55‾

44)   67
    × 10

45)   46
    × 1,000

46)   64
    × 100

47)   29
    × 10

48)   96
    × 100

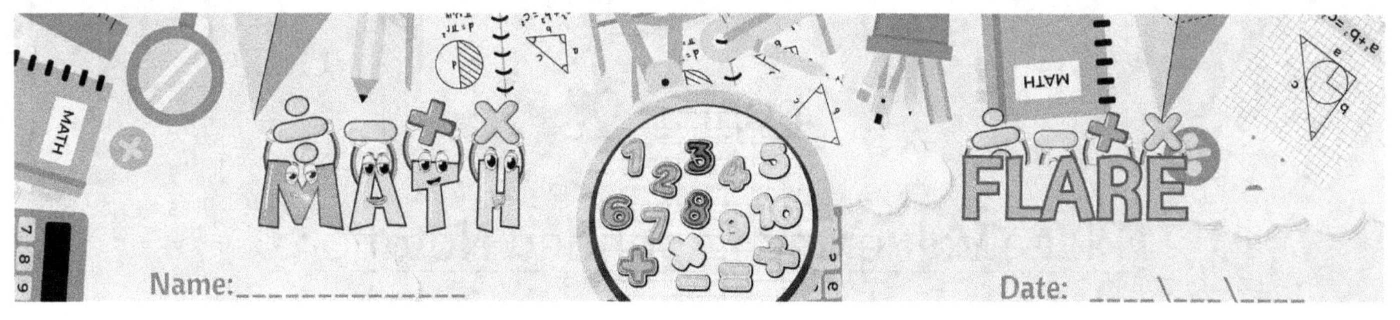

49) 10) 87

50) 10) 30

51) 100) 51

52) 100) 97

53)
20
× 100

54)
20
× 10

55) 100) 56

56) 1,000) 94

57) 10) 51

58)
44
× 10

59) 10) 40

60)
71
× 10

61) 1,000) 70

62)
62
× 100

63) 100) 88

64)
69
× 1,000

Chapter. 02

Place Value and Expanded Notations

Place value tells us the value of a digit in a number based on where it's placed.

Imagine we have the number 987,647.528. It has 9 digits.

Now, each digit holds a special place. Let's break down the number 987,647.528:

- The digit 9 is in the hundred thousands place. Its value is 9×100,000=900,000.

- The digit 8 is in the ten thousands place. Its value is 8×10,000=80,000.

- The digit 7 is in the thousands place. Its value is 7×1,000=7,000.

- The digit 6 is in the hundreds place. Its value is 6×100=600.

- The digit 4 is in the tens place. Its value is 4×10=40.

- The digit 7 is in the ones place. Its value is 7×1=7.

- The digit 5 is in the tenths place. Its value is $5 \times \frac{1}{10} = 0.5$.

- The digit 2 is in the hundredths place. Its value is $2 \times \frac{1}{100} = 0.02$.

- The digit 8 is in the thousandths place. Its value is $8 \times \frac{1}{1000} = 0.008$.

When we add these values together, we find the value of the entire number:

$$900,000 + 80,000 + 7,000 + 600 + 40 + 7 + 0.5 + 0.02 + 0.008 = 987,647.528$$

Let's solve some problems:

Place value of the underlined digit:

$$78,865,761 = \underline{\qquad 6 \text{ tens} \qquad}$$

Expanded notations:

| 175,596.19 | 100,000 + 70,000 + 5,000 + 500 + 90 + 6 + 0.1 + 0.09 |

8,684,690.5 — 8 millions + 6 hundred thousands + 8 ten thousands + 4 thousands + 6 hundreds + 9 tens + 5 tenths

192,883.30 — 1 hundred thousand + 9 ten thousands + 2 thousands + 8 hundreds + 8 tens + 3 ones + 3 tenths

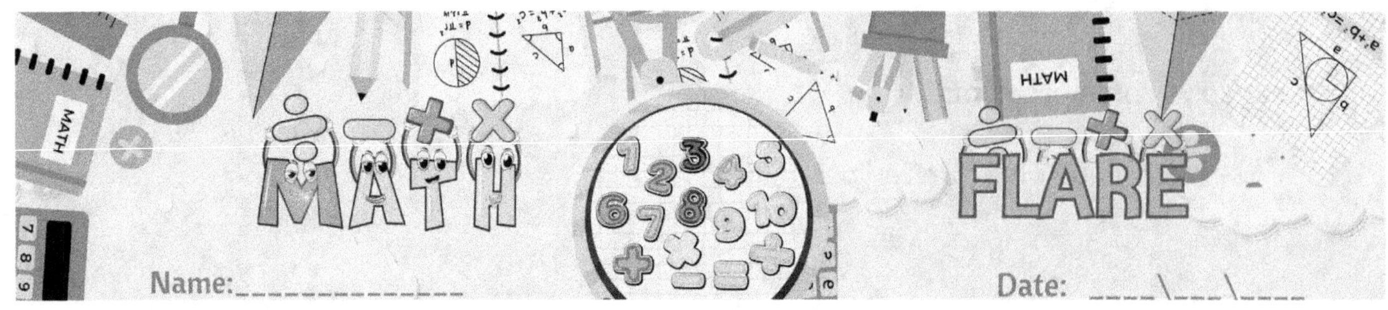

Place Value

Determine the place value of the underlined digit.

1) 78,865,7_61 = _6 tens_

2) 28,556,_577 = _______________________

3) 2,9_53,582.2 = _______________________

4) _48,652,755 = _______________________

5) 9,476,1_99.7 = _______________________

6) 358,1_31.69 = _______________________

7) 65,626,_298 = _______________________

8) 1,121,509.5 = _______________________

9) 43,994.634 = _______________________

10) 65,798,915 = _______________________

11) 28,539,802 = _______________________

12) 95,531,174 = _______________________

13) 190,705.15 = _______________________

14) 4,176,129.8 = _______________________

15) 760,568.55 = _______________________

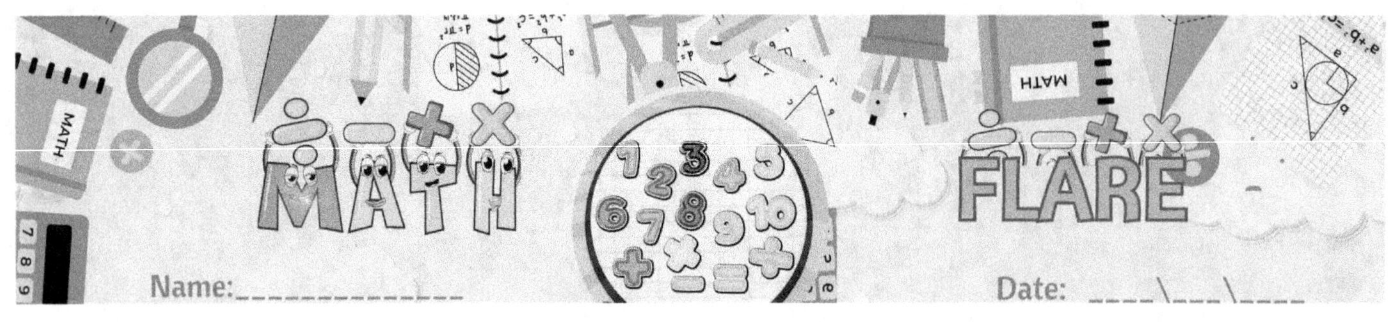

16) 901,433.4 = _______________________________

17) 98,283.685 = _______________________________

18) 7,940,961.1 = _______________________________

19) 295,260.09 = _______________________________

20) 4,276,175.3 = _______________________________

21) 238,103.72 = _______________________________

22) 779,186.17 = _______________________________

23) 3,897,249.8 = _______________________________

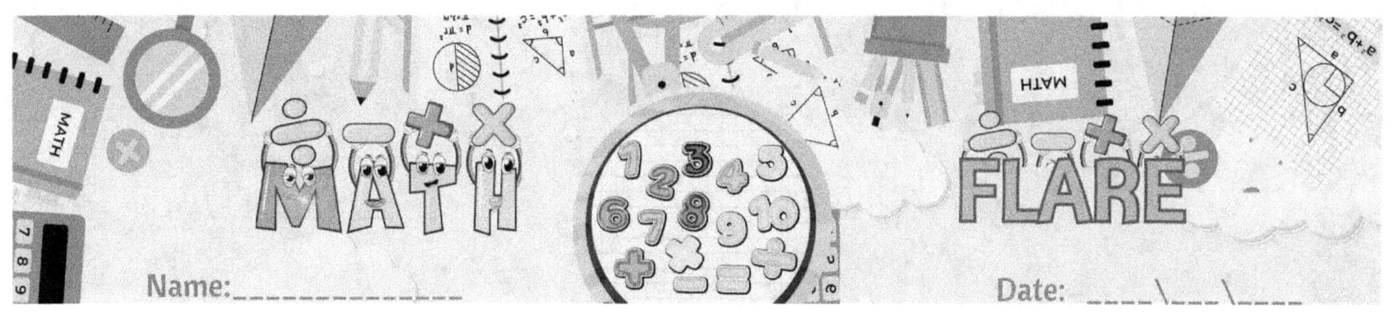

24) 95,703,74<u>2</u> = ________________________

25) 52,474.20<u>2</u> = ________________________

26) 85,087.<u>7</u>85 = ________________________

27) 14,<u>4</u>57,045 = ________________________

28) 6,972,<u>7</u>16.5 = ________________________

29) <u>2</u>5,984,049 = ________________________

30) 9,641,<u>9</u>16.2 = ________________________

31) 75,713.62<u>1</u> = ________________________

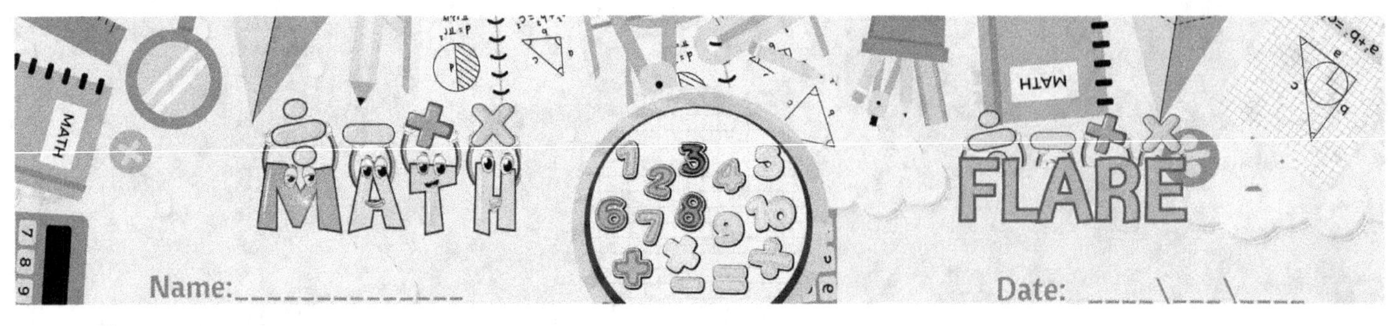

32) 11,607.904 = _________________________________

33) 40,628,693 = _________________________________

34) 3,744,397.9 = _________________________________

35) 18,506,762 = _________________________________

36) 111,670.43 = _________________________________

37) 91,353.709 = _________________________________

38) 131,652.03 = _________________________________

39) 1,303,702.6 = _________________________________

Place Value and Expanded Notation

1) _175,596.19_ 100,000 + 70,000 + 5,000 + 500 + 90 + 6 + 0.1 + 0.09

2) _______________ 20,000,000 + 1,000,000 + 500,000 + 80,000 + 2,000 + 900 + 60 + 4

3) _______________ 60,000 + 7,000 + 500 + 20 + 1 + 0.6 + 0.03

4) _______________ 10,000 + 6,000 + 900 + 80 + 6 + 0.6 + 0.05

5) _______________ 9,000,000 + 300,000 + 30,000 + 6,000 + 200 + 80 + 1 + 0.3

6) _______________ 60,000,000 + 2,000,000 + 500,000 + 50,000 + 5,000 + 400 + 10 + 6

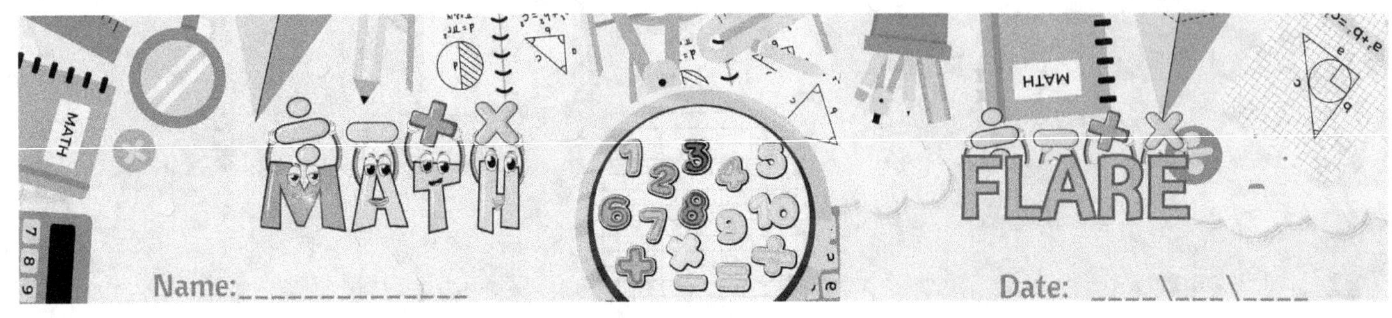

7) _________________________ $800,000 + 70 + 8 + 0.5 + 0.07$

8) _________________________ $30,000,000 + 3,000,000 + 900,000 + 50,000 + 8,000 + 200 + 70 + 2$

9) _________________________ $70,000,000 + 4,000,000 + 600,000 + 10,000 + 3,000 + 600 + 30 + 1$

10) _________________________ $40,000,000 + 9,000,000 + 70,000 + 5,000 + 800 + 40 + 1$

11) _________________________ $500,000 + 50,000 + 1,000 + 600 + 80 + 0.5 + 0.02$

12) _________________________ $5,000,000 + 90,000 + 5,000 + 40 + 8 + 0.1$

13) _________________________ $100,000 + 20,000 + 1,000 + 700 + 80 + 8 + 0.7 + 0.03$

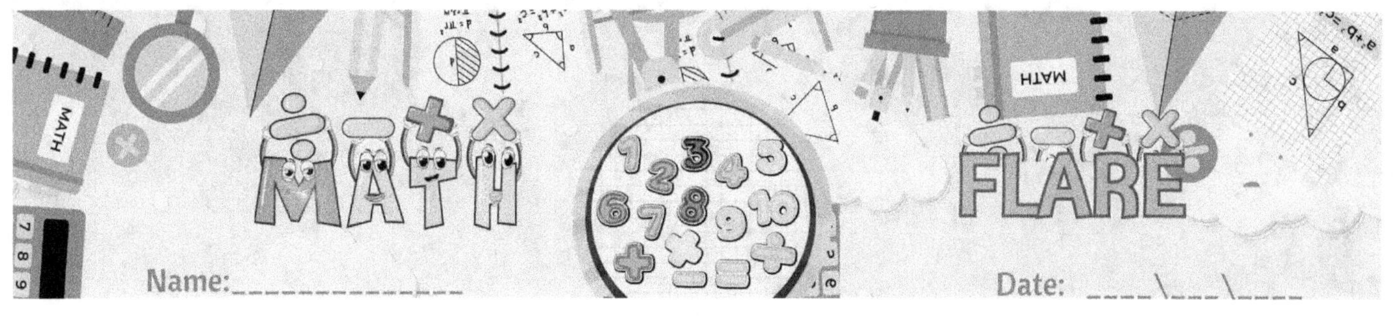

14) _________________________ $80{,}000 + 6{,}000 + 300 + 90 + 2 + 0.2 + 0.01 + 0.006$

15) _________________________ $900{,}000 + 30{,}000 + 2{,}000 + 600 + 30 + 5 + 0.6 + 0.02$

16) _________________________ $50{,}000 + 1{,}000 + 90 + 2 + 0.07 + 0.003$

17) _________________________ $70{,}000{,}000 + 7{,}000{,}000 + 800{,}000 + 80{,}000 + 8{,}000 + 500 + 3$

18) _________________________ $2{,}000{,}000 + 400{,}000 + 50{,}000 + 9{,}000 + 200 + 3 + 0.9$

19) _________________________ $9{,}000{,}000 + 700{,}000 + 80{,}000 + 4{,}000 + 700 + 20 + 6 + 0.6$

20) _________________________ $80{,}000 + 8{,}000 + 700 + 90 + 4 + 0.7 + 0.03$

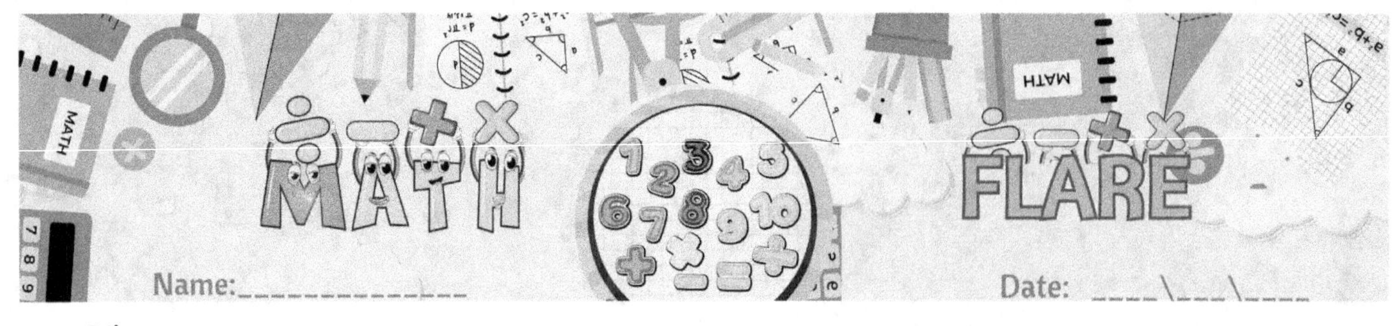

21) _________________________   500,000 + 10,000 + 100 + 90

22) _________________________   400,000 + 50,000 + 2,000 + 100 + 70 + 6 + 0.2 + 0.09

23) _________________________   80,000,000 + 9,000,000 + 700,000 + 70,000 + 2,000 + 700 + 10 + 6

24) _________________________   10,000,000 + 200,000 + 20,000 + 8,000 + 200 + 80 + 7

25) _________________________   50,000,000 + 9,000,000 + 500,000 + 50,000 + 7,000 + 300 + 10 + 3

26) _________________________   10,000 + 8,000 + 300 + 90 + 1 + 0.8 + 0.03 + 0.005

27) _________________________   300,000 + 60,000 + 5,000 + 400 + 50 + 8 + 0.3 + 0.01

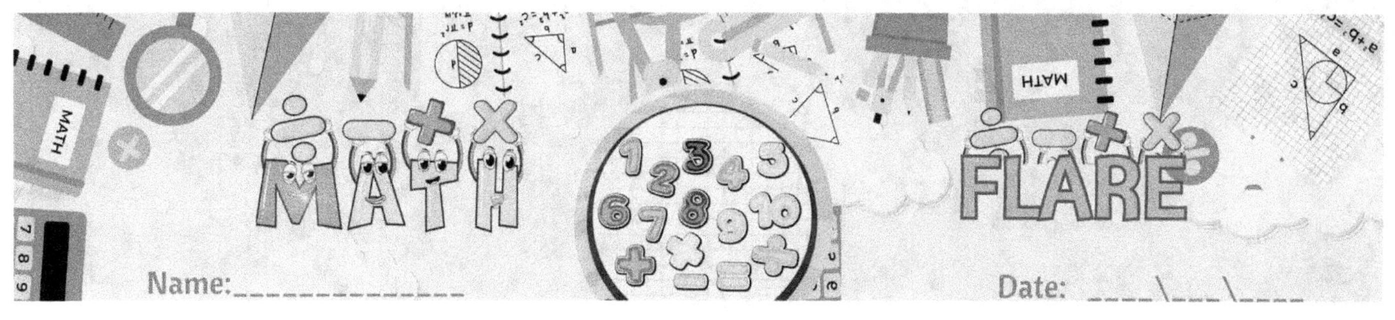

28) _________________________ 90,000,000 + 4,000,000 + 300,000 + 20,000 + 5,000 + 300 + 40 + 3

29) _________________________ 10,000 + 9,000 + 100 + 20 + 8 + 0.7

30) _________________________ 20,000 + 4,000 + 100 + 60 + 3 + 0.2 + 0.09 + 0.006

31) _________________________ 10,000,000 + 5,000,000 + 300,000 + 30,000 + 6,000 + 200 + 90 + 7

32) _________________________ 50,000,000 + 8,000,000 + 700,000 + 80,000 + 5,000 + 700 + 20 + 8

33) _________________________ 700,000 + 90,000 + 9,000 + 200 + 30 + 2 + 0.8 + 0.02

34) _________________________ 900,000 + 90,000 + 8,000 + 200 + 20 + 6 + 0.09

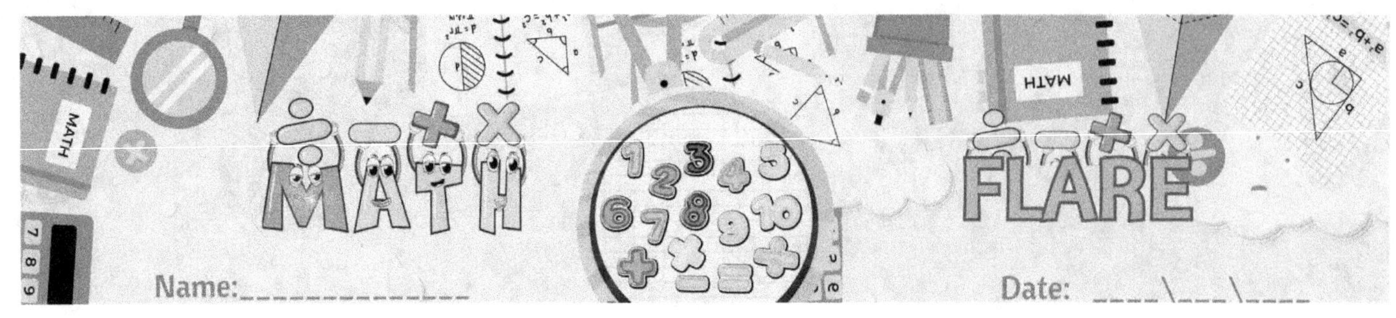

35) _________________________   200,000 + 50,000 + 6,000 + 900 + 40 + 9 + 0.1 + 0.07

36) _________________________   60,000,000 + 3,000,000 + 300,000 + 6,000 + 800 + 40 + 8

37) _________________________   400,000 + 10,000 + 2,000 + 600 + 80

38) _________________________   80,000,000 + 8,000,000 + 100,000 + 30,000 + 1,000 + 800 + 30 + 3

39) _________________________   80,000 + 3,000 + 9 + 0.7 + 0.07 + 0.001

40) _________________________   800,000 + 30,000 + 500 + 90 + 0.5 + 0.01

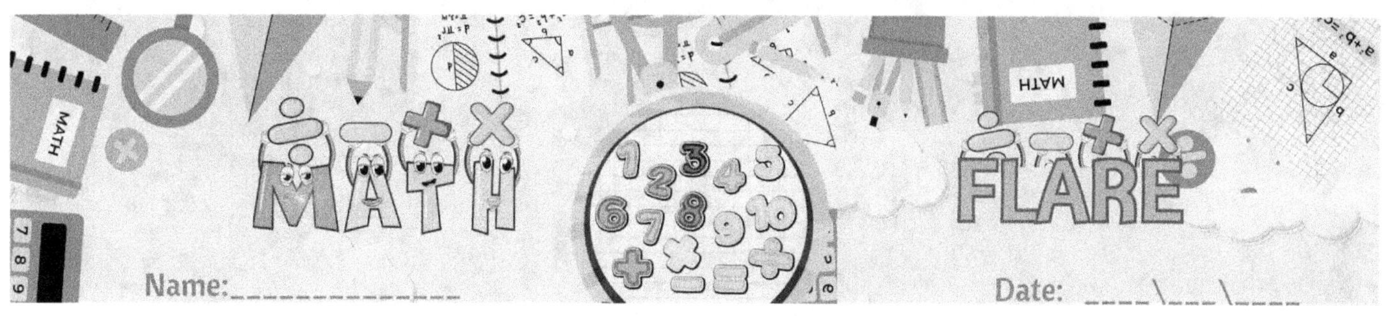

Place Value and Expanded Notation

1)   **8,684,690.5**   8 millions + 6 hundred thousands + 8 ten thousands + 4 thousands + 6 hundreds + 9 tens + 5 tenths

2) ____________________ 8 millions + 6 ten thousands + 6 thousands + 2 hundreds + 7 tens + 8 ones

3) ____________________ 9 hundred thousands + 1 ten thousand + 1 thousand + 1 hundred + 5 tens + 8 ones + 8 tenths + 1 hundredth

4) ____________________ 6 hundred thousands + 7 thousands + 3 hundreds + 5 tens + 5 ones + 2 tenths

5) ________________________ 7 ten thousands + 8 thousands + 4 hundreds + 3 tens + 5 ones + 7 tenths + 3 hundredths + 9 thousandths

6) ________________________ 9 ten thousands + 5 thousands + 6 hundreds + 7 tens + 7 tenths + 5 hundredths + 7 thousandths

7) ________________________ 9 ten millions + 9 millions + 1 hundred thousand + 3 thousands + 5 hundreds + 3 ones

8) ________________________ 1 ten thousand + 8 thousands + 4 hundreds + 1 ten + 8 ones + 7 hundredths + 6 thousandths

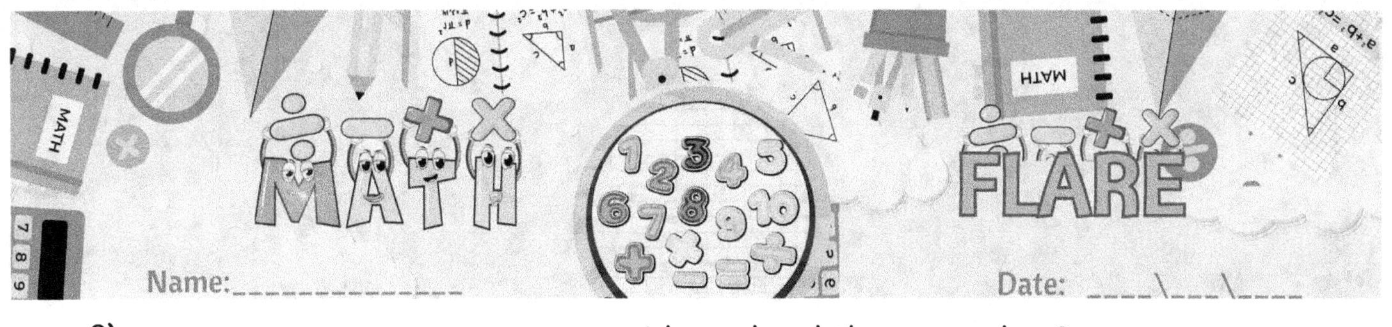

9) _________________________ 1 hundred thousand + 8 ten thousands + 3 thousands + 1 hundred + 2 ones + 2 tenths + 6 hundredths

10) _________________________ 3 millions + 5 hundred thousands + 1 thousand + 2 tens + 7 ones + 1 tenth

11) _________________________ 5 ten millions + 5 millions + 5 hundred thousands + 2 ten thousands + 3 thousands + 6 hundreds + 7 tens + 1 one

12) _________________________ 7 ten millions + 1 hundred thousand + 5 ten thousands + 6 thousands + 9 hundreds + 5 tens + 6 ones

13) _________________________ 7 hundred thousands + 2 thousands + 9 hundreds + 8 tens + 9 ones + 1 hundredth

14) _________________________ 9 millions + 6 hundred thousands + 1 ten thousand + 8 thousands + 4 hundreds + 4 tens + 6 ones + 6 tenths

15) _________________________ 4 ten millions + 7 hundred thousands + 8 ten thousands + 4 thousands + 9 hundreds + 2 tens + 5 ones

16) _________________________ 7 hundred thousands + 2 ten thousands + 3 thousands + 4 hundreds + 1 ten + 9 ones + 8 tenths + 8 hundredths

17) _________________________________   3 ten thousands + 1 thousand + 8 hundreds + 1 ten + 2 tenths + 4 hundredths + 7 thousandths

18) _________________________________   6 ten thousands + 7 thousands + 2 hundreds + 9 tens + 3 ones + 3 tenths + 4 hundredths + 3 thousandths

19) _________________________________   5 ten millions + 7 millions + 4 hundred thousands + 2 ten thousands + 9 thousands + 3 hundreds + 3 tens + 6 ones

20) _________________________________   8 ten millions + 4 millions + 9 hundred thousands + 7 ten thousands + 9 hundreds + 7 tens + 8 ones

21) _______________________ 3 ten millions + 6 millions + 9 thousands + 5 hundreds + 8 tens + 5 ones

22) _______________________ 8 hundred thousands + 5 ten thousands + 6 thousands + 8 hundreds + 2 tens + 5 ones + 1 tenth + 3 hundredths

23) _______________________ 2 hundred thousands + 4 ten thousands + 8 thousands + 2 hundreds + 9 tens + 5 ones + 7 tenths + 3 hundredths

24) _______________________ 6 ten millions + 4 hundred thousands + 5 ten thousands + 3 hundreds + 3 tens + 6 ones

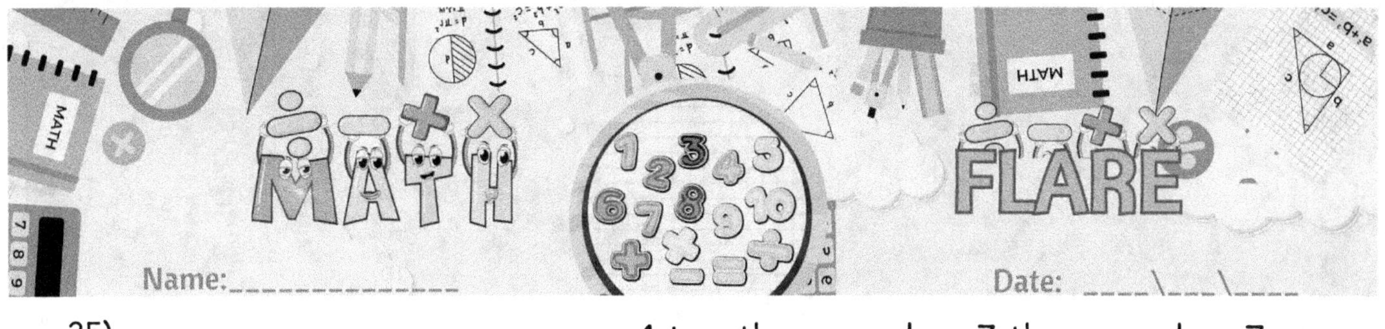

25) _________________________ 4 ten thousands + 3 thousands + 7 hundreds + 3 tens + 9 ones + 5 tenths + 4 hundredths + 4 thousandths

26) _________________________ 9 millions + 6 hundred thousands + 3 ten thousands + 8 thousands + 2 hundreds + 3 tens + 2 ones + 4 tenths

27) _________________________ 7 millions + 1 hundred thousand + 2 thousands + 7 hundreds + 1 ten + 9 ones + 8 tenths

28) _________________________ 1 million + 2 hundred thousands + 3 ten thousands + 5 thousands + 6 hundreds + 2 tens + 6 ones + 3 tenths

29) ______________________ 7 hundred thousands + 6 thousands + 9 hundreds + 7 tens + 2 ones + 9 tenths + 9 hundredths

30) ______________________ 3 millions + 9 hundred thousands + 9 ten thousands + 5 thousands + 6 hundreds + 7 tens + 1 one + 4 tenths

31) ______________________ 1 ten million + 9 millions + 8 hundred thousands + 2 ten thousands + 4 thousands + 7 tens + 4 ones

32) ______________________ 8 hundred thousands + 9 ten thousands + 7 thousands + 5 hundreds + 6 tens + 6 ones + 6 tenths + 9 hundredths

33) _________________________________ 4 ten thousands + 1 thousand + 5 hundreds + 8 tens + 2 ones + 2 tenths + 6 hundredths + 7 thousandths

34) _________________________________ 2 ten thousands + 4 thousands + 7 hundreds + 8 tens + 8 ones + 2 tenths + 1 hundredth + 6 thousandths

35) _________________________________ 1 million + 1 hundred thousand + 9 ten thousands + 4 thousands + 7 hundreds + 8 tens + 2 ones + 6 tenths

36) _________________________________ 7 millions + 3 ten thousands + 5 thousands + 6 hundreds + 2 tens + 1 one + 8 tenths

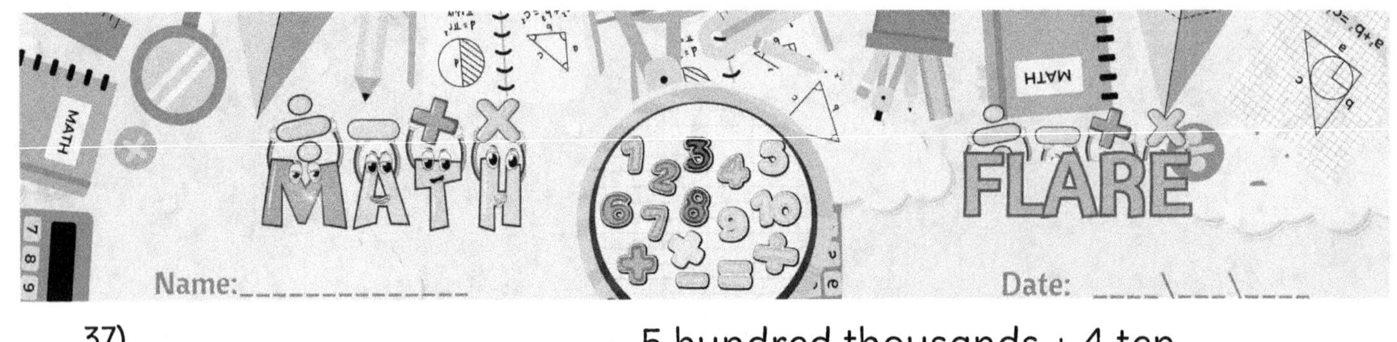

37) _______________________ 5 hundred thousands + 4 ten thousands + 1 thousand + 1 ten + 7 ones + 4 tenths + 7 hundredths

38) _______________________ 3 ten millions + 9 millions + 3 ten thousands + 7 thousands + 1 hundred + 9 tens + 6 ones

39) _______________________ 3 ten thousands + 1 thousand + 7 hundreds + 9 tens + 2 ones + 5 tenths + 4 hundredths + 6 thousandths

40) _______________________ 6 millions + 3 hundred thousands + 8 ten thousands + 8 thousands + 6 hundreds + 5 tens + 5 ones + 5 tenths

Place Value and Expanded Notation

1) 192,883.30   1 hundred thousand + 9 ten thousands
+ 2   thousands + 8 hundreds + 8 tens
+ 3 ones + 3   tenths

2) 2,812,775.5

3) 860,151.16

4) 84,118.427

5) 6,863,962.4 ______________________

6) 451,793.40 ______________________

7) 88,486,826 ______________________

8) 8,373,881.5 ______________________

9) 690,376.83 ______________________

10) 53,352.928 _______________________________

11) 414,966.02 _______________________________

12) 739,746.55 _______________________________

13) 4,070,249.7 _______________________________

14) 9,803,879.2 _______________________________

15) 57,049.466 _______________________________

____

____

16) 111,643.92 _______________________________

____

____

17) 6,583,320.8 _______________________________

____

____

18) 406,655.45 _______________________________

____

____

19) 2,699,597.6 _______________________________

____

____

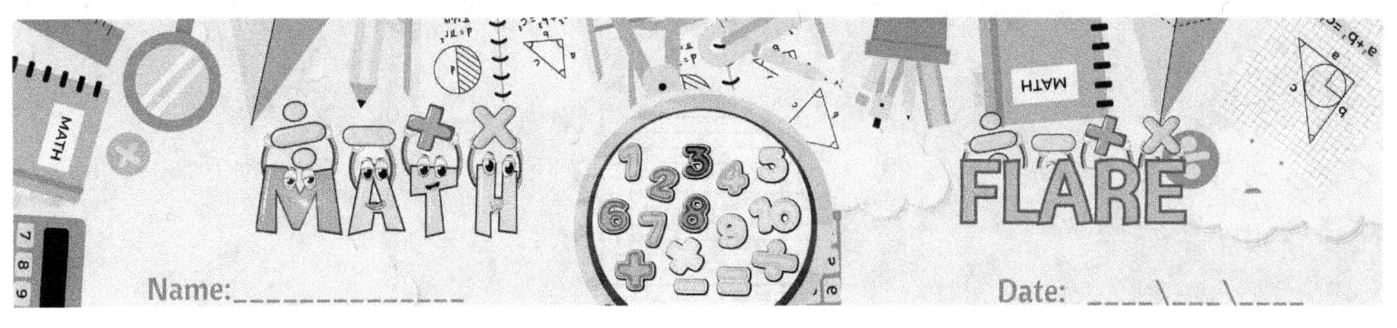

20) 8,205,341.5 ___________________________

____

____

21) 34,643.559 ___________________________

____

____

22) 96,747,240 ___________________________

____

____

23) 47,720,776 ___________________________

____

____

24) 78,353,511 ___________________________

____

____

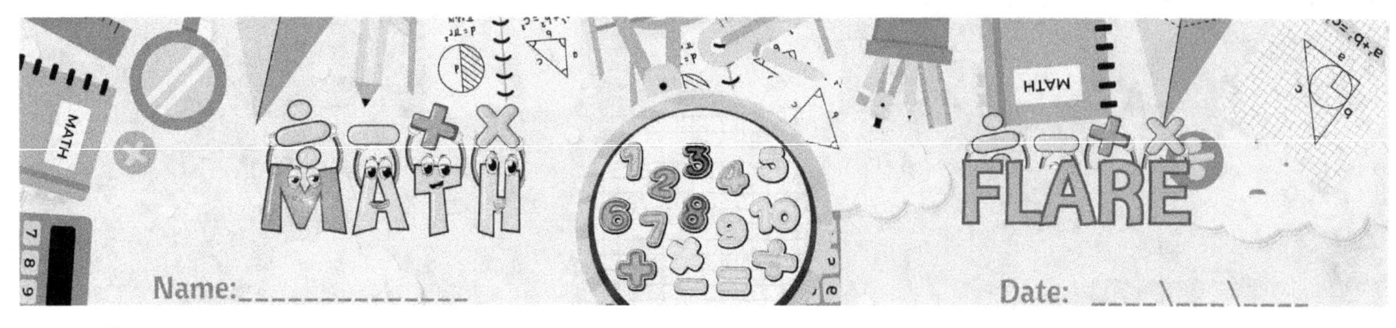

25) 2,518,619.8

26) 65,767,002

27) 385,746.89

28) 55,510,685

29) 94,236.641

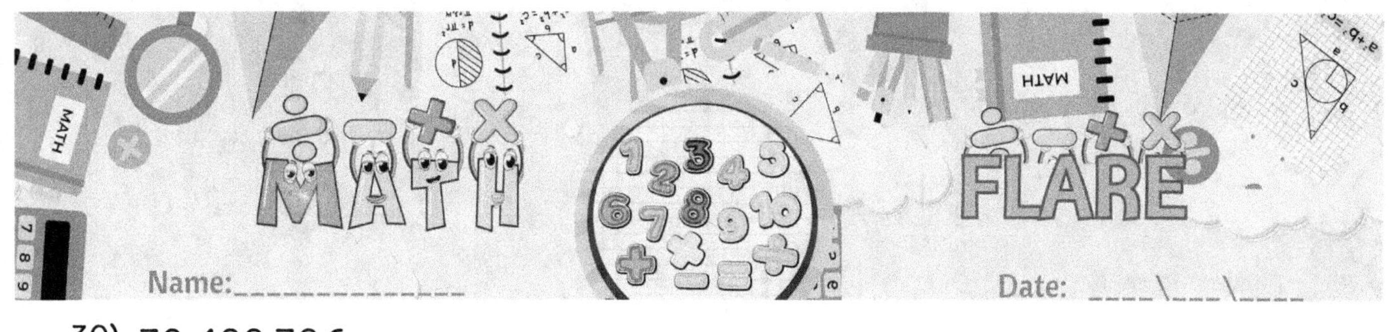

30) 70,428.706 ______________________

31) 282,402.41 ______________________

32) 92,773.050 ______________________

33) 455,007.97 ______________________

34) 935,427.80 ______________________

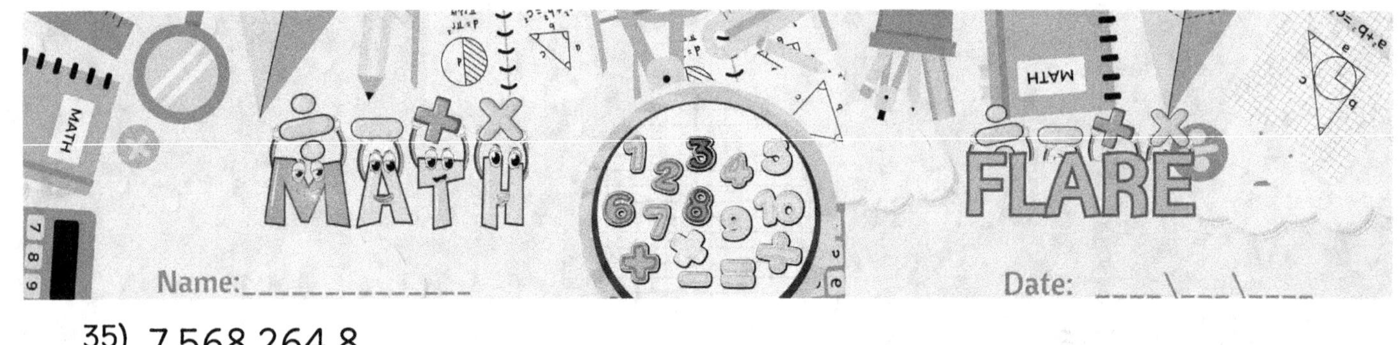

35) 7,568,264.8 _______________________________________
____
____

36) 1,788,183.0 _______________________________________
____
____

37) 99,667,396 _______________________________________
____
____

38) 4,071,114.4 _______________________________________
____
____

39) 918,107.11 _______________________________________
____
____

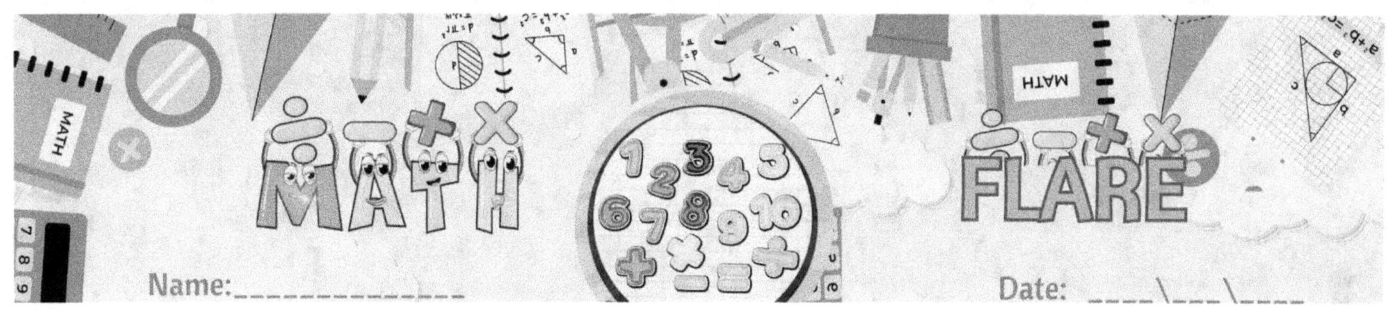

Lowest Common Multiple

Find the lowest common multiple.

1) 8   8, 16, 24, 32, 40, 48, 56   56
    7   7, 14, 21, 28, 35, 42, 49, 56

2) 7
    8

3) 4
    8

4) 6
    5

5) 7
    5

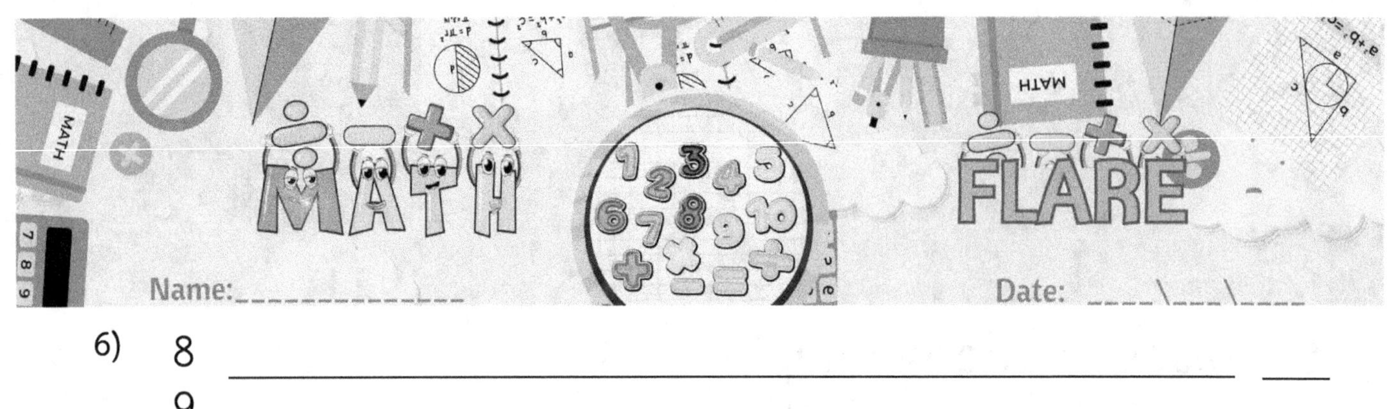

6)   8
     9

7)   4
     3

8)   3
     2

9)   5
     8

10) 10
     7

11) 9
     8

12) 9
    5 _______________________________ ____

13) 8
    5 _______________________________ ____

14) 5
    9 _______________________________ ____

15) 2
    4 _______________________________ ____

16) 5
    3 _______________________________ ____

17) 3
    5 _______________________________ ____

18) 10
    6 ____ ____

19) 2
     5 ____ ____

20) 3
    10 ____ ____

21) 4
     7 ____ ____

22) 3
     8 ____ ____

23) 2
     8 ____ ____

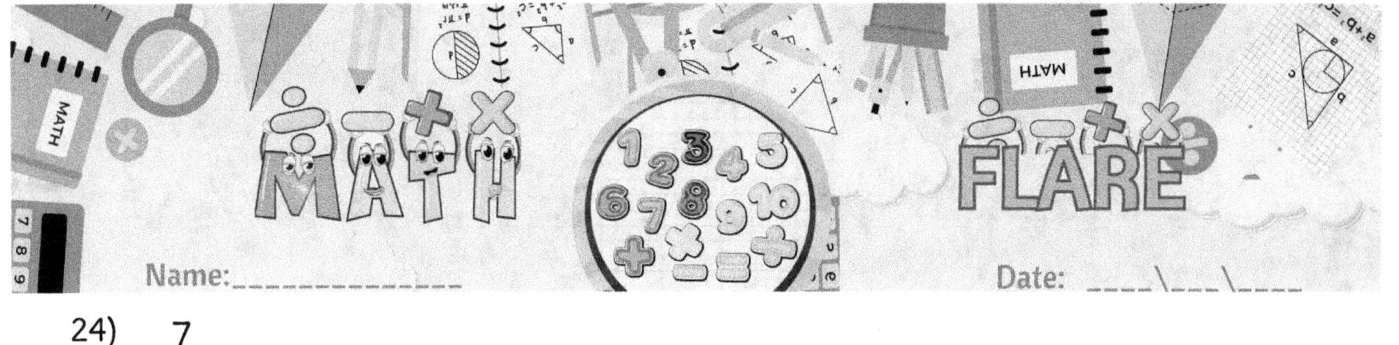

24) 7
     10   ____

25) 4
     5   ____

26) 3
     9   ____

27) 2
     6   ____

28) 6
     7   ____

29) 7
     2   ____

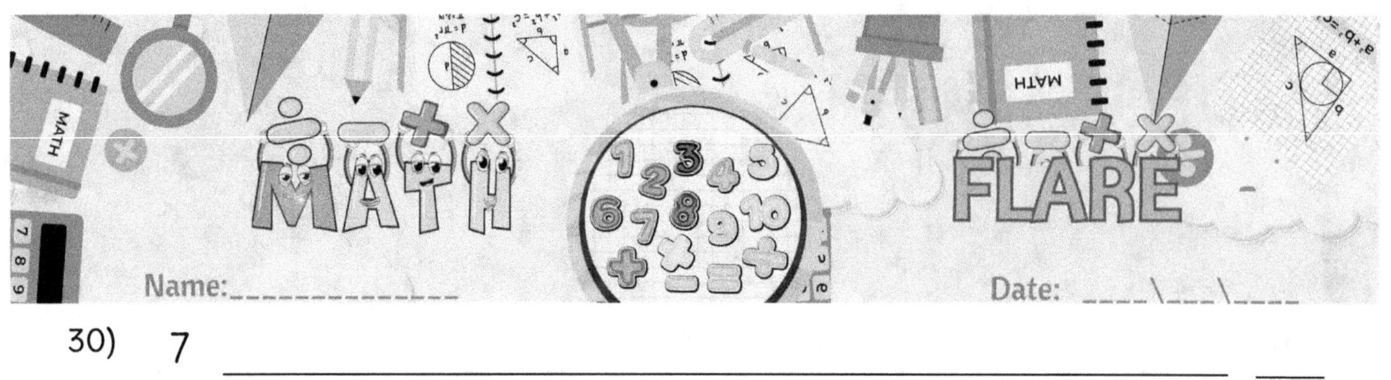

30) 7
     3

31) 5
     7

32) 10
     9

33) 10
     8

34) 4
     9

35) 5
     2

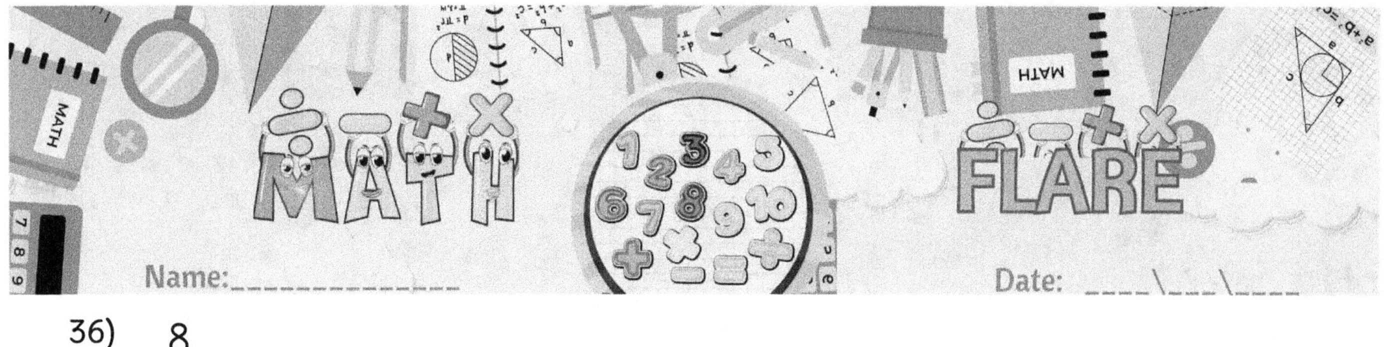

36) 8
     2   ___

37) 5
     6   ___

38) 8
     6   ___

39) 7
     4   ___

40) 3
     7   ___

41) 6
     2   ___

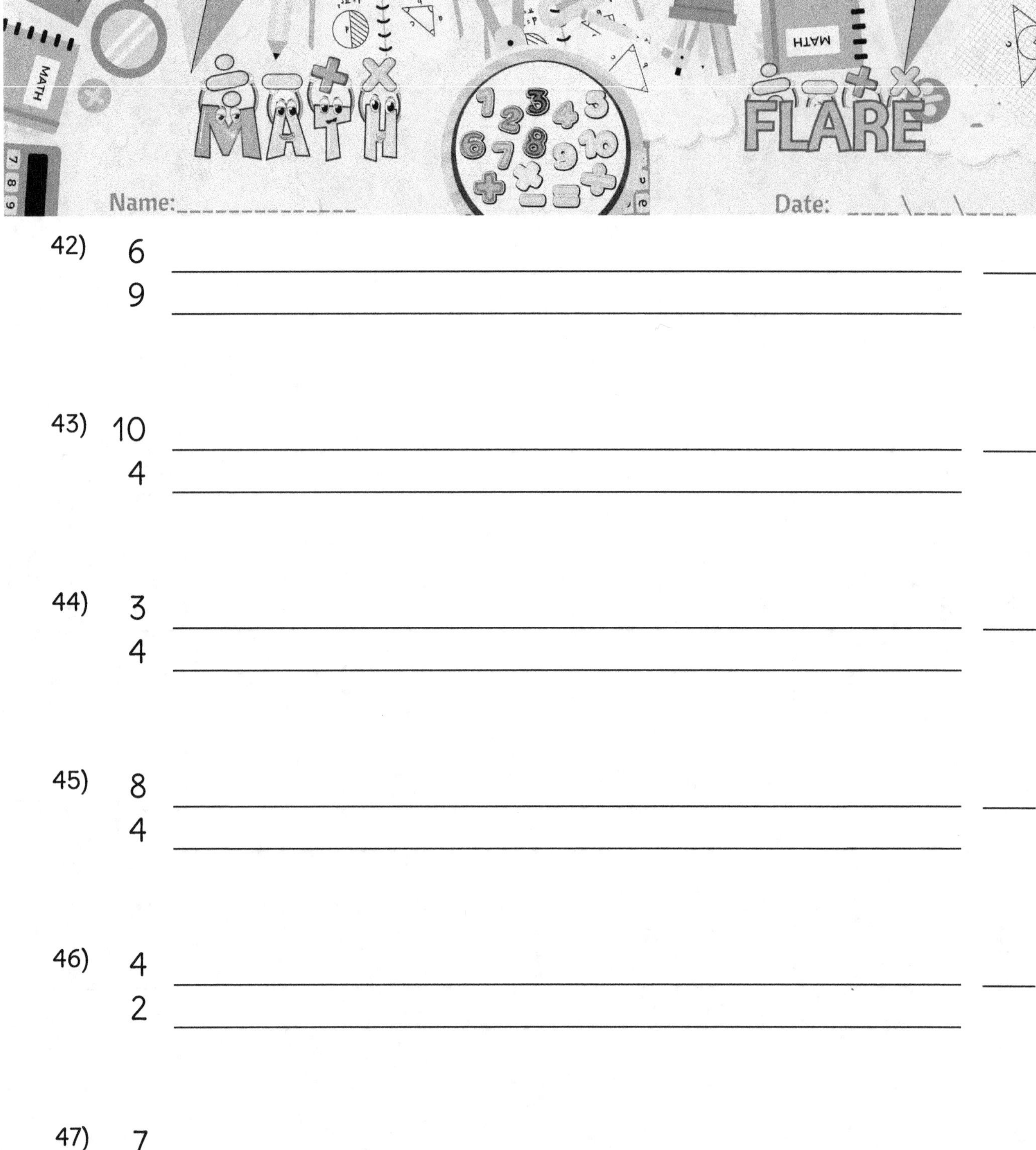

42) 6
     9

43) 10
     4

44) 3
     4

45) 8
     4

46) 4
     2

47) 7
     9

Chapter. 05

Fractions

Fractions represent parts of a whole. They consist of a numerator (the number on top) and a denominator (the number on the bottom).

For example: we have an orange, and we divide it into 5 equal slices. Each slice represents $\frac{1}{5}$ of the orange. Now, if we take 3 of those slices, we have taken $\frac{3}{5}$ of the orange.

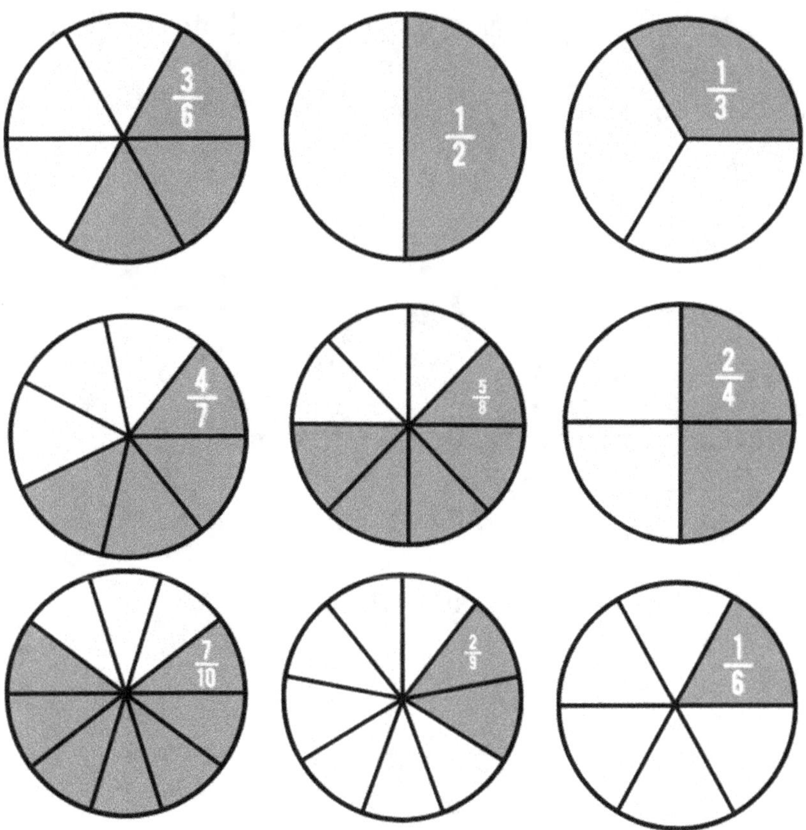

Equivalent Fractions

Equivalent fractions are fractions that represent the same value or part of a whole, even though they may look different.

To find equivalent fractions, you can:

- Multiply or divide both the numerator and denominator by the same nonzero number.
- Simplify fractions to their simplest form.

$\frac{1}{2}$ and $\frac{2}{4}$ are equivalent fractions because if you multiply the numerator and denominator of $\frac{1}{2}$ by 2, you get $\frac{2}{4}$. Similarly, if you divide both the numerator and denominator of $\frac{2}{4}$ by 2, you get $\frac{1}{2}$.

Let's solve a problem:

$$\frac{}{8} = \frac{15}{40}$$

To solve the missing numerator, we can cross multiply.

$$40x = 8 \times 15$$

$$40x = 120$$

$$x = \frac{120}{40} = x = 3$$

$$\frac{3}{8} = \frac{15}{40}$$

Least Common Multiple (LCM)

The Lowest Common Multiple (LCM) of two or more numbers is the smallest multiple that is divisible by each of the numbers.

There are several methods to find the LCM; however, we will focus on only two:

Listing Multiples: List the multiples of each number until you find a common multiple. For example:

$$
\begin{array}{r|l}
8 & 8,\ 16,\ 24,\ 32,\ 40,\ 48,\ 56 \\
\hline
7 & 7,\ 14,\ 21,\ 28,\ 35,\ 42,\ 49,\ 56
\end{array}
$$

, LCM = $\underline{56}$

Division Method: Divide each number with the smallest prime number that divides at least one of the numbers evenly. The product of all the divisors and quotients is the LCM. For example:

$$
\begin{array}{c|cc}
2 & 7 & 8 \\
\hline
2 & 7 & 4 \\
\hline
2 & 7 & 2 \\
\hline
7 & 7 & 1 \\
\hline
  & 1 & 1
\end{array}
$$

$$\text{LCM} = 2 \times 2 \times 2 \times 7 = \underline{56}$$

Both methods have their advantages. For big numbers, using the division way is usually faster. But if we are working with smaller numbers or like seeing patterns, listing multiples might make more sense.

Fractions Addition (Uncommon Denominator)

When adding fractions with uncommon denominators, we need to find a common denominator before we can add them. We will follow the following steps:

1. **Find the Least Common Denominator (LCD).** Determine the least common multiple (LCM) of the denominators.
2. **Convert fractions to have the common denominator** : Rewrite each fraction so that it has the common denominator found in step 1. To do this, multiply the numerator and denominator of each fraction by the same value to make the denominators the same.
3. **Add the fractions:** Once the fractions have the same denominator, add the numerators together and keep the denominator the same.
4. **Simplify, if necessary:** If possible, simplify the resulting fraction by reducing it to its simplest form.

For example, let's add:

$$\frac{5}{11} + \frac{1}{4}$$

The LCM = 2 x 2 x 11 = <u>44</u>

$$\frac{5x4 + 1x11}{11x4} = \frac{20 + 11}{44}$$

$$\frac{31}{44}$$

Fractions Subtraction (Uncommon Denominator)

Fractions subtraction with uncommon denominator follows the same steps except that we subtract instead of adding the fractions.

For example:

$$\frac{5}{11} - \frac{1}{4}$$

$$\text{The LCM} = 2 \times 2 \times 11 = \underline{44}$$

$$\frac{5 \times 4 - 1 \times 11}{11 \times 4} = \frac{20 - 11}{44}$$

$$\frac{9}{44}$$

Fractions Multiplication

To multiply fractions, we simply multiply the numerators together to get the new numerator and multiply the denominators together to get the new denominator.

For example, let's multiply: $\frac{2}{4} \times \frac{1}{4}$

$$\text{Numerator: } 2 \times 1 = 2$$

$$\text{Denominator: } 4 \times 4 = 16$$

$$\text{Therefore, } \frac{2}{16}$$

$$\text{we can simplify the resulting fraction: } \frac{1}{8}$$

Let's solve a problem:

$$\frac{4}{5} \times \frac{4}{5} = \frac{4 \times 4}{5 \times 5} = \frac{16}{25}$$

Fractions Division

To divide fractions, we multiply by the reciprocal of the divisor.

For example, let's divide:

$$\frac{6}{8} \div \frac{4}{8}$$

$$\frac{6}{8} \times \frac{8}{4} = \frac{48}{32} = \frac{3}{2}$$

Fractions Addition Word Problems

Aria spent $\frac{1}{3}$ of her salary on watches and then $\frac{1}{2}$ of the money on food. How much money did she spend?

$$\frac{1}{3} + \frac{1}{2} = \frac{2 \times 1 + 3 \times 1}{3 \times 2} = \frac{2 + 3}{6} = \frac{5}{6} \qquad \text{she spent } \frac{5}{6} \text{ of her money}$$

Fractions Subtraction Word Problems

A container has $\frac{2}{5}$ of a gallon of milk. If $\frac{2}{6}$ of the milk is taken out and put into another container, how much milk is left in the original container in gallons?

$$\frac{2}{5} - \frac{2}{6} = \frac{2 \times 6 + 2 \times 5}{5 \times 6} = \frac{12 - 10}{30} = \frac{2}{30} = \frac{1}{15}$$

there is $\frac{1}{15}$ gallons of milk is left in original container.

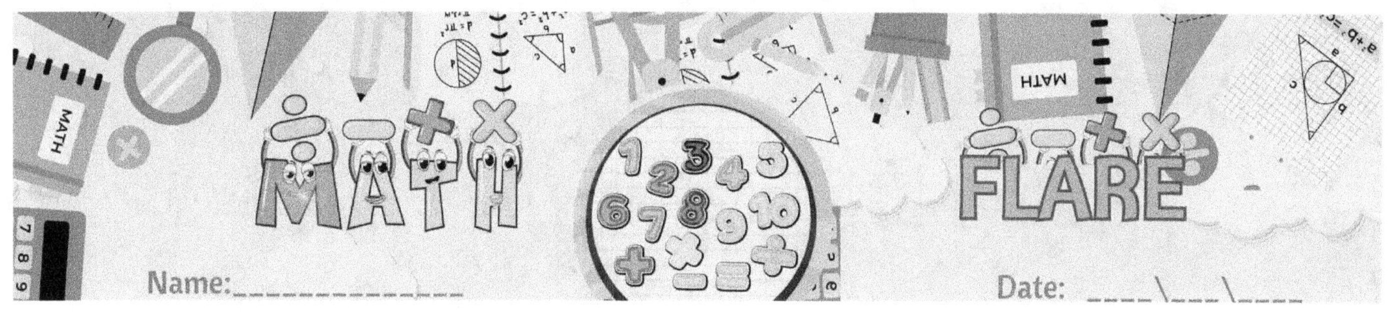

Equivalent Fractions

1) $\dfrac{4}{9} = \dfrac{32}{72}$

2) $\dfrac{3}{} = \dfrac{9}{24}$

3) $\dfrac{17}{19} = \dfrac{136}{}$

4) $\dfrac{}{16} = \dfrac{25}{80}$

5) $\dfrac{1}{} = \dfrac{8}{16}$

6) $\dfrac{12}{} = \dfrac{84}{105}$

7) $\dfrac{15}{} = \dfrac{45}{51}$

8) $\dfrac{9}{10} = \dfrac{72}{}$

9) $\dfrac{2}{} = \dfrac{8}{20}$

10) $\dfrac{3}{} = \dfrac{27}{54}$

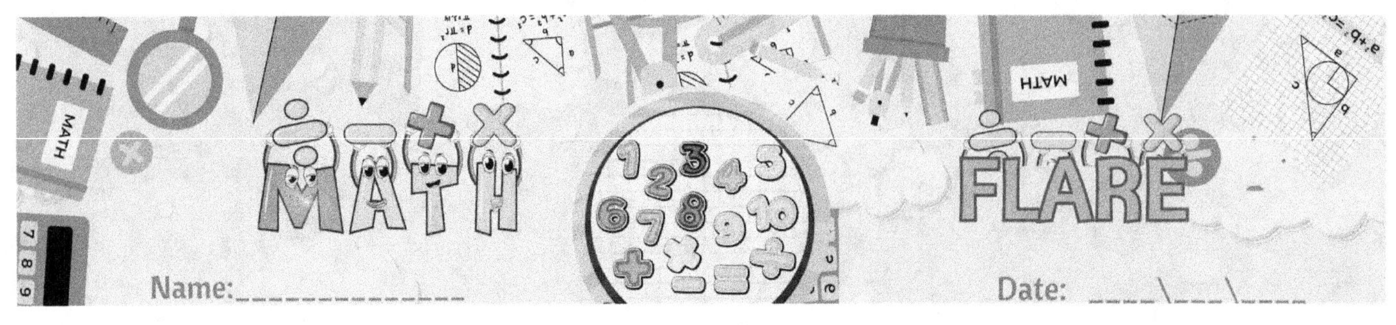

11) $\dfrac{}{11} = \dfrac{16}{88}$

12) $\dfrac{}{18} = \dfrac{28}{36}$

13) $\dfrac{11}{} = \dfrac{33}{39}$

14) $\dfrac{2}{4} = \dfrac{20}{}$

15) $\dfrac{9}{} = \dfrac{90}{140}$

16) $\dfrac{3}{4} = \dfrac{}{32}$

17) $\dfrac{2}{12} = \dfrac{}{60}$

18) $\dfrac{11}{15} = \dfrac{55}{}$

19) $\dfrac{2}{} = \dfrac{6}{9}$

20) $\dfrac{2}{7} = \dfrac{}{56}$

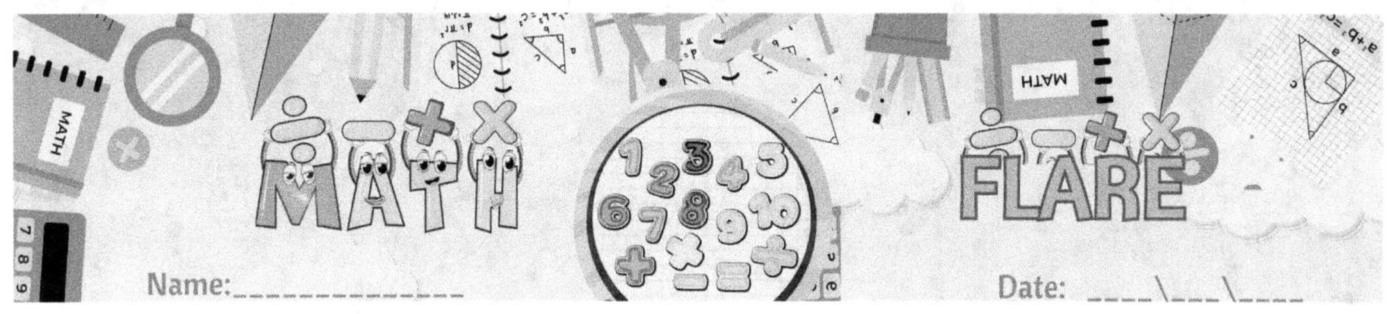

21) $\dfrac{1}{2} = \dfrac{}{12}$

22) $\dfrac{}{19} = \dfrac{18}{57}$

23) $\dfrac{}{18} = \dfrac{8}{72}$

24) $\dfrac{3}{} = \dfrac{12}{44}$

25) $\dfrac{2}{10} = \dfrac{}{40}$

26) $\dfrac{}{8} = \dfrac{35}{56}$

27) $\dfrac{8}{9} = \dfrac{}{90}$

28) $\dfrac{}{13} = \dfrac{21}{39}$

29) $\dfrac{}{17} = \dfrac{135}{153}$

30) $\dfrac{5}{6} = \dfrac{15}{}$

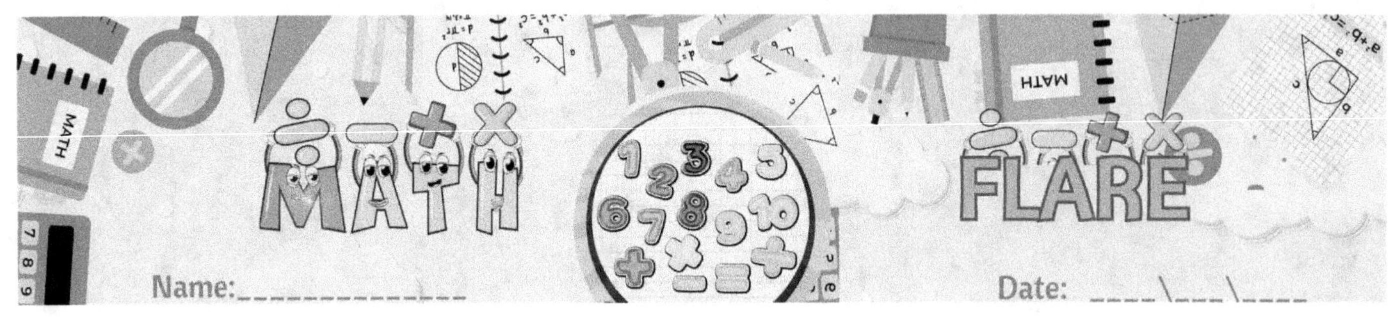

31) $\dfrac{4}{} = \dfrac{8}{10}$

32) $\dfrac{7}{20} = \dfrac{}{40}$

33) $\dfrac{1}{16} = \dfrac{5}{}$

34) $\dfrac{8}{} = \dfrac{24}{39}$

35) $\dfrac{3}{15} = \dfrac{30}{}$

36) $\dfrac{6}{11} = \dfrac{}{110}$

37) $\dfrac{}{3} = \dfrac{4}{6}$

38) $\dfrac{}{14} = \dfrac{28}{56}$

39) $\dfrac{}{4} = \dfrac{10}{40}$

40) $\dfrac{15}{20} = \dfrac{}{120}$

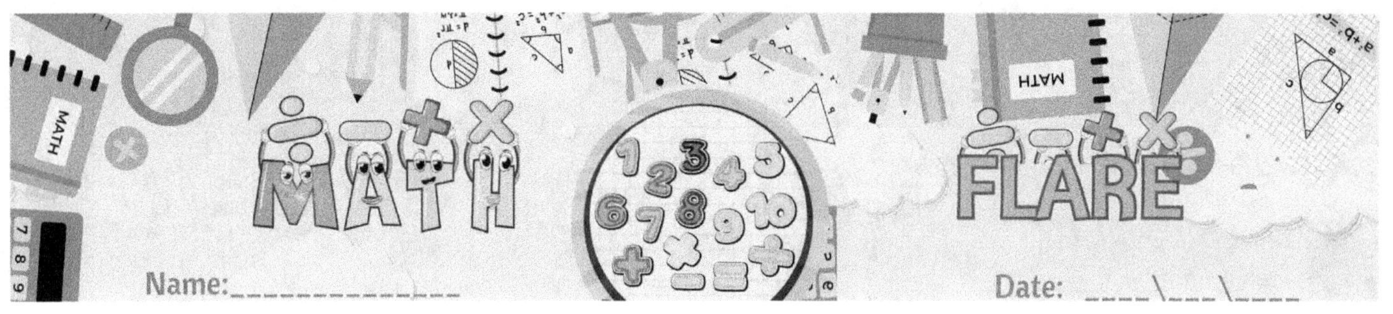

41) $\dfrac{3}{12} = \dfrac{9}{}$

42) $\dfrac{16}{17} = \dfrac{80}{}$

43) $\dfrac{}{2} = \dfrac{7}{14}$

44) $\dfrac{}{18} = \dfrac{30}{108}$

45) $\dfrac{6}{7} = \dfrac{12}{}$

46) $\dfrac{2}{9} = \dfrac{18}{}$

47) $\dfrac{2}{} = \dfrac{6}{15}$

48) $\dfrac{4}{10} = \dfrac{}{90}$

49) $\dfrac{14}{} = \dfrac{28}{38}$

50) $\dfrac{13}{} = \dfrac{117}{144}$

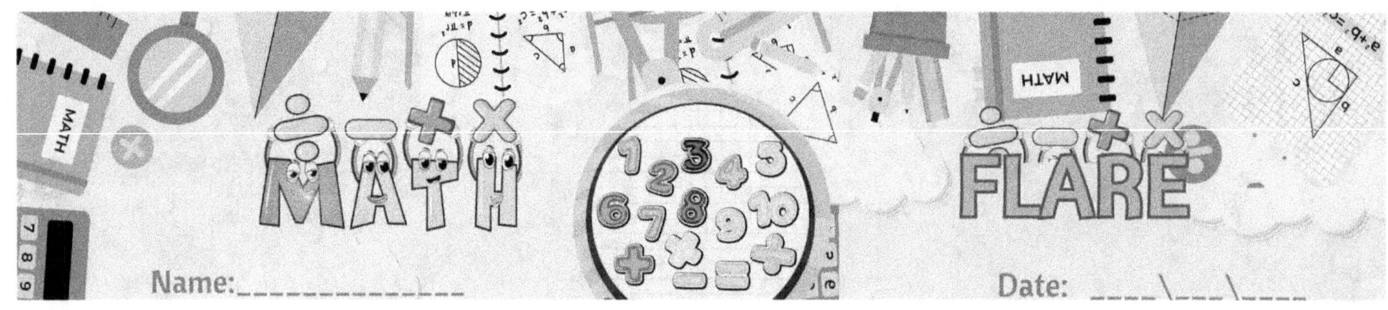

Fractions Addition: Uncommon Denominator

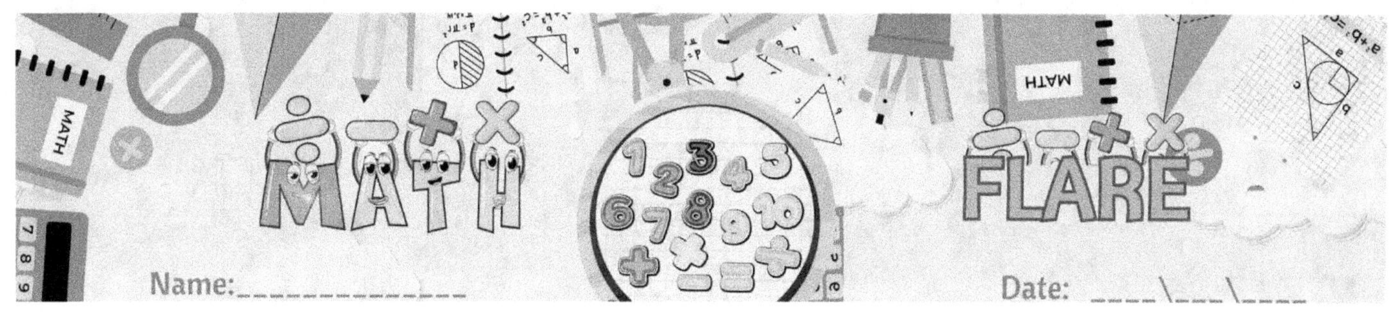

11) $\dfrac{2}{12} + \dfrac{1}{8} =$ ______________

12) $\dfrac{1}{3} + \dfrac{1}{7} =$ ______________

13) $\dfrac{1}{4} + \dfrac{9}{19} =$ ______________

14) $\dfrac{1}{13} + \dfrac{3}{10} =$ ______________

15) $\dfrac{2}{6} + \dfrac{3}{18} =$ ______________

16) $\dfrac{2}{5} + \dfrac{1}{13} =$ ______________

17) $\dfrac{1}{2} + \dfrac{2}{14} =$ ______________

18) $\dfrac{9}{14} + \dfrac{1}{4} =$ ______________

19) $\dfrac{5}{9} + \dfrac{7}{20} =$ ______________

20) $\dfrac{14}{18} + \dfrac{1}{14} =$ ______________

21) $\dfrac{2}{7} + \dfrac{2}{11} =$ ______________

22) $\dfrac{2}{10} + \dfrac{11}{15} =$ ______________

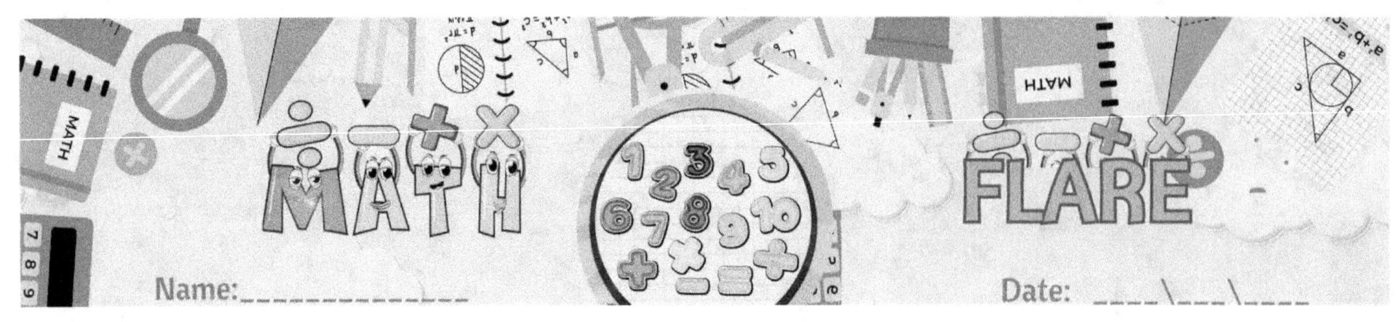

23) $\dfrac{5}{15} + \dfrac{10}{18} =$ ____________

24) $\dfrac{1}{3} + \dfrac{2}{5} =$ ____________

25) $\dfrac{1}{2} + \dfrac{3}{10} =$ ____________

26) $\dfrac{3}{16} + \dfrac{1}{8} =$ ____________

27) $\dfrac{6}{11} + \dfrac{3}{12} =$ ____________

28) $\dfrac{13}{20} + \dfrac{4}{16} =$ ____________

29) $\dfrac{9}{18} + \dfrac{1}{3} =$ ____________

30) $\dfrac{1}{5} + \dfrac{6}{20} =$ ____________

31) $\dfrac{1}{16} + \dfrac{1}{14} =$ ____________

32) $\dfrac{2}{17} + \dfrac{3}{13} =$ ____________

33) $\dfrac{1}{10} + \dfrac{6}{16} =$ ____________

34) $\dfrac{1}{6} + \dfrac{3}{11} =$ ____________

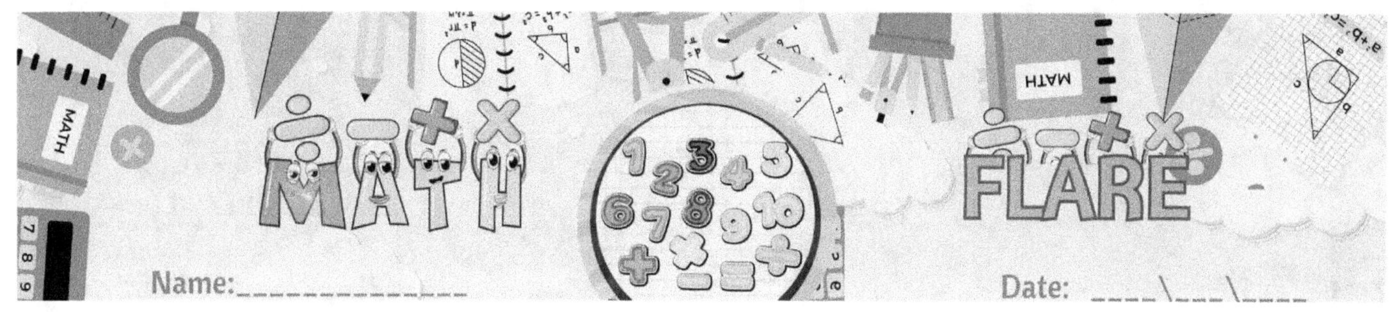

35) $\dfrac{2}{9} + \dfrac{1}{2} =$ _______________

36) $\dfrac{1}{4} + \dfrac{2}{4} =$ _______________

37) $\dfrac{1}{3} + \dfrac{1}{5} =$ _______________

38) $\dfrac{6}{7} + \dfrac{1}{9} =$ _______________

39) $\dfrac{5}{15} + \dfrac{6}{13} =$ _______________

40) $\dfrac{9}{19} + \dfrac{3}{18} =$ _______________

41) $\dfrac{2}{8} + \dfrac{2}{12} =$ _______________

42) $\dfrac{16}{20} + \dfrac{1}{19} =$ _______________

43) $\dfrac{1}{18} + \dfrac{4}{17} =$ _______________

44) $\dfrac{1}{5} + \dfrac{3}{5} =$ _______________

45) $\dfrac{2}{6} + \dfrac{7}{16} =$ _______________

46) $\dfrac{1}{2} + \dfrac{1}{4} =$ _______________

47) $\dfrac{1}{4} + \dfrac{1}{2} =$ _______________

48) $\dfrac{1}{7} + \dfrac{2}{3} =$ _______________

49) $\dfrac{1}{15} + \dfrac{5}{20} =$ _______________

50) $\dfrac{9}{13} + \dfrac{2}{7} =$ _______________

51) $\dfrac{1}{2} + \dfrac{1}{16} =$ _______________

52) $\dfrac{3}{7} + \dfrac{3}{8} =$ _______________

53) $\dfrac{4}{10} + \dfrac{2}{10} =$ _______________

54) $\dfrac{2}{8} + \dfrac{3}{13} =$ _______________

55) $\dfrac{1}{4} + \dfrac{1}{17} =$ _______________

56) $\dfrac{1}{3} + \dfrac{1}{3} =$ _______________

57) $\dfrac{4}{17} + \dfrac{2}{4} =$ _______________

58) $\dfrac{1}{9} + \dfrac{2}{5} =$ _______________

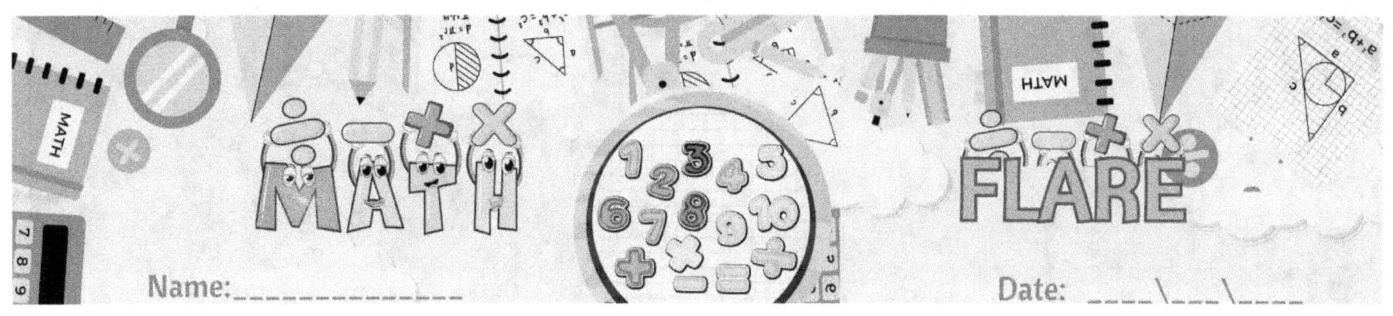

Fractions Subtraction: (Uncommon Denominator)

Find the difference.

1) $\dfrac{10}{17} - \dfrac{1}{2} = \dfrac{3}{34}$

$\dfrac{10\times2 - 1\times17}{17\times2} = \dfrac{20 - 17}{34}$

2) $\dfrac{11}{13} - \dfrac{5}{17} =$ _______________

3) $\dfrac{7}{10} - \dfrac{4}{9} =$ _______________

4) $\dfrac{3}{13} - \dfrac{3}{17} =$ _______________

5) $\dfrac{14}{15} - \dfrac{3}{16} =$ _______________

6) $\dfrac{12}{20} - \dfrac{1}{2} =$ _______________

7) $\dfrac{6}{11} - \dfrac{4}{13} =$ _______________

8) $\dfrac{10}{14} - \dfrac{4}{6} =$ _______________

9) $\dfrac{1}{2} - \dfrac{5}{14} =$ _______________

10) $\dfrac{14}{16} - \dfrac{3}{11} =$ _______________

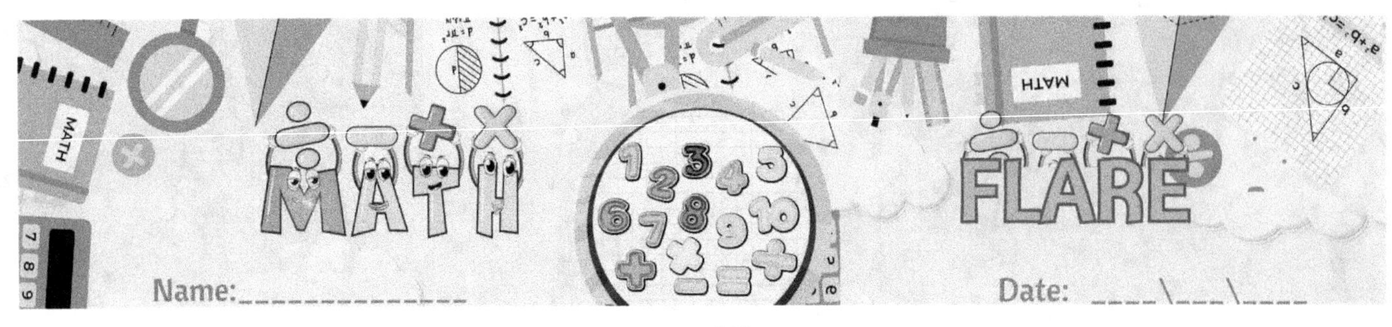

11) $\dfrac{3}{4} - \dfrac{1}{10} =$ _______________

12) $\dfrac{1}{2} - \dfrac{2}{9} =$ _______________

13) $\dfrac{8}{9} - \dfrac{1}{2} =$ _______________

14) $\dfrac{14}{19} - \dfrac{9}{14} =$ _______________

15) $\dfrac{7}{14} - \dfrac{6}{19} =$ _______________

16) $\dfrac{1}{2} - \dfrac{1}{3} =$ _______________

17) $\dfrac{15}{17} - \dfrac{1}{2} =$ _______________

18) $\dfrac{11}{16} - \dfrac{4}{6} =$ _______________

19) $\dfrac{4}{6} - \dfrac{3}{15} =$ _______________

20) $\dfrac{8}{10} - \dfrac{8}{19} =$ _______________

21) $\dfrac{3}{4} - \dfrac{6}{13} =$ _______________

22) $\dfrac{7}{8} - \dfrac{2}{6} =$ _______________

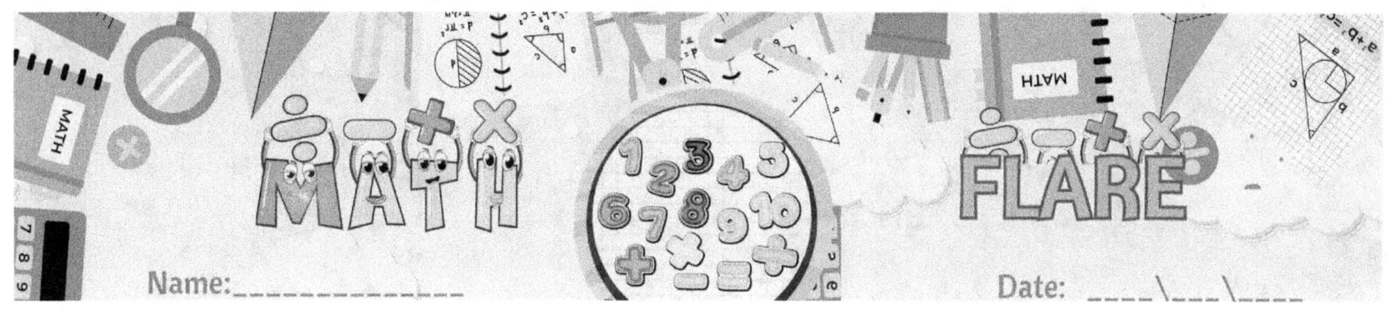

23) $\dfrac{6}{12} - \dfrac{1}{3} =$ ________________

24) $\dfrac{3}{6} - \dfrac{3}{10} =$ ________________

25) $\dfrac{16}{17} - \dfrac{2}{15} =$ ________________

26) $\dfrac{4}{5} - \dfrac{1}{8} =$ ________________

27) $\dfrac{5}{6} - \dfrac{7}{13} =$ ________________

28) $\dfrac{6}{12} - \dfrac{1}{7} =$ ________________

29) $\dfrac{16}{17} - \dfrac{1}{13} =$ ________________

30) $\dfrac{12}{14} - \dfrac{4}{6} =$ ________________

31) $\dfrac{9}{18} - \dfrac{2}{5} =$ ________________

32) $\dfrac{3}{5} - \dfrac{8}{16} =$ ________________

33) $\dfrac{6}{13} - \dfrac{1}{9} =$ ________________

34) $\dfrac{3}{9} - \dfrac{3}{15} =$ ________________

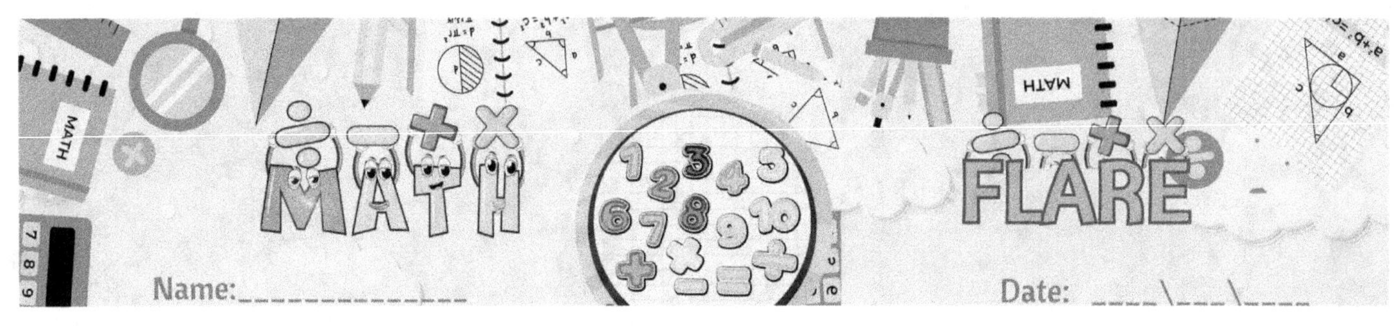

35) $\dfrac{5}{6} - \dfrac{1}{4} =$ ______________

36) $\dfrac{17}{19} - \dfrac{10}{13} =$ ______________

37) $\dfrac{1}{2} - \dfrac{2}{20} =$ ______________

38) $\dfrac{8}{12} - \dfrac{6}{14} =$ ______________

39) $\dfrac{5}{10} - \dfrac{7}{18} =$ ______________

40) $\dfrac{6}{8} - \dfrac{10}{16} =$ ______________

41) $\dfrac{6}{15} - \dfrac{4}{13} =$ ______________

42) $\dfrac{12}{13} - \dfrac{3}{15} =$ ______________

43) $\dfrac{6}{10} - \dfrac{10}{17} =$ ______________

44) $\dfrac{1}{2} - \dfrac{2}{6} =$ ______________

45) $\dfrac{2}{5} - \dfrac{1}{9} =$ ______________

46) $\dfrac{12}{16} - \dfrac{5}{15} =$ ______________

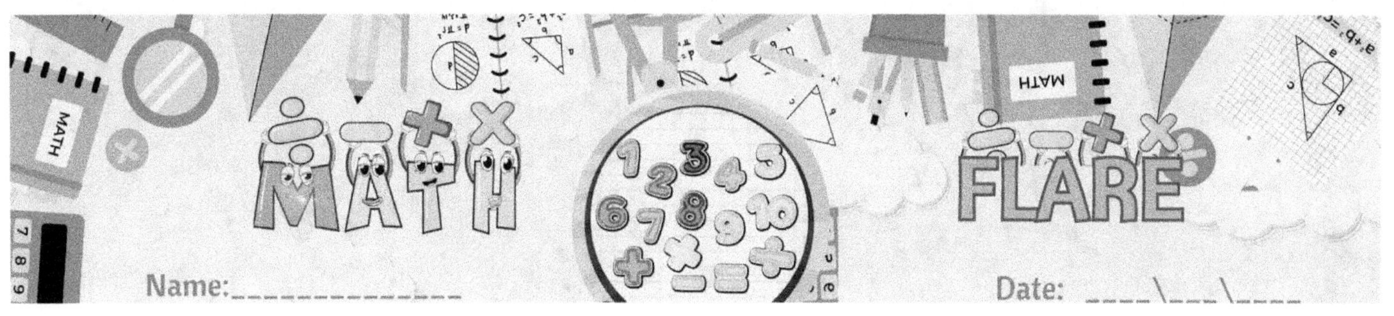

47) $\dfrac{11}{19} - \dfrac{1}{7} =$ _______________

48) $\dfrac{6}{9} - \dfrac{2}{11} =$ _______________

49) $\dfrac{2}{3} - \dfrac{1}{2} =$ _______________

50) $\dfrac{7}{8} - \dfrac{2}{4} =$ _______________

51) $\dfrac{12}{15} - \dfrac{10}{19} =$ _______________

52) $\dfrac{11}{18} - \dfrac{5}{12} =$ _______________

53) $\dfrac{8}{9} - \dfrac{3}{5} =$ _______________

54) $\dfrac{5}{6} - \dfrac{11}{18} =$ _______________

55) $\dfrac{3}{19} - \dfrac{1}{11} =$ _______________

56) $\dfrac{3}{7} - \dfrac{6}{15} =$ _______________

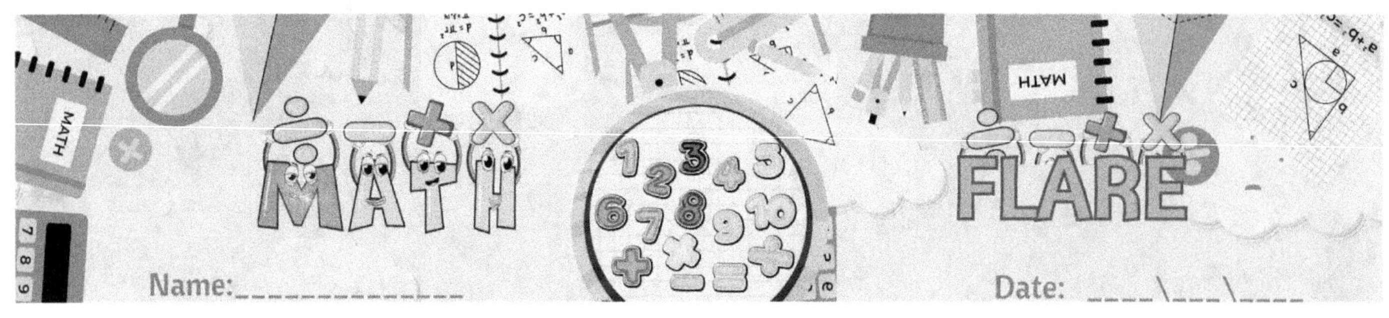

Fractions Multiplication

Find the product.

1) $\dfrac{1}{3} \times \dfrac{4}{5} =$ ______ $\dfrac{4}{15}$

$\dfrac{1 \times 4}{3 \times 5}$

2) $\dfrac{2}{3} \times \dfrac{1}{6} =$ ______

3) $\dfrac{5}{11} \times \dfrac{8}{9} =$ ______

4) $\dfrac{1}{6} \times \dfrac{1}{2} =$ ______

5) $\dfrac{2}{3} \times \dfrac{1}{2} =$ ______

6) $\dfrac{3}{4} \times \dfrac{1}{4} =$ ______

7) $\dfrac{2}{3} \times \dfrac{2}{11} =$ ______

8) $\dfrac{1}{3} \times \dfrac{4}{9} =$ ______

9) $\dfrac{7}{8} \times \dfrac{1}{2} =$ ______

10) $\dfrac{5}{6} \times \dfrac{1}{6} =$ ______

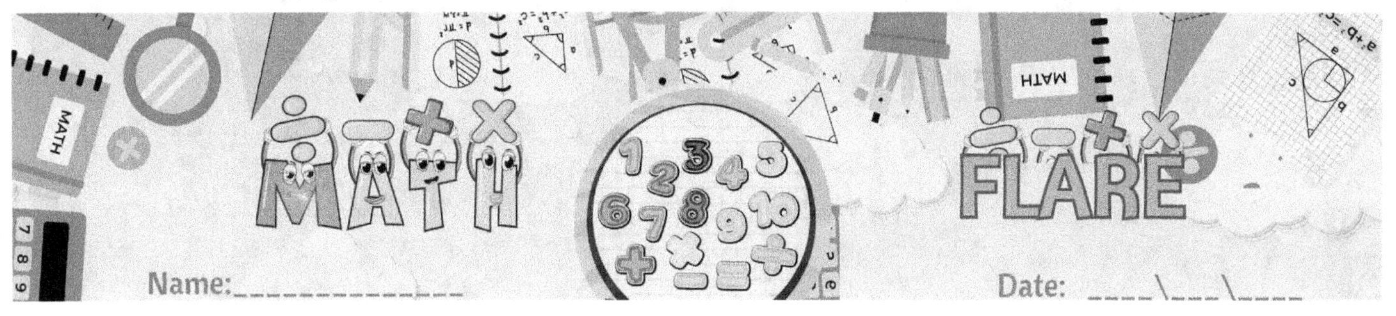

11) $\dfrac{2}{7} \times \dfrac{1}{9} =$ _________________

12) $\dfrac{1}{3} \times \dfrac{2}{7} =$ _________________

13) $\dfrac{1}{3} \times \dfrac{1}{3} =$ _________________

14) $\dfrac{4}{11} \times \dfrac{2}{3} =$ _________________

15) $\dfrac{2}{5} \times \dfrac{8}{9} =$ _________________

16) $\dfrac{1}{6} \times \dfrac{3}{8} =$ _________________

17) $\dfrac{9}{11} \times \dfrac{1}{2} =$ _________________

18) $\dfrac{2}{7} \times \dfrac{1}{7} =$ _________________

19) $\dfrac{5}{6} \times \dfrac{1}{2} =$ _________________

20) $\dfrac{1}{2} \times \dfrac{2}{5} =$ _________________

21) $\dfrac{1}{8} \times \dfrac{1}{2} =$ _________________

22) $\dfrac{1}{2} \times \dfrac{3}{4} =$ _________________

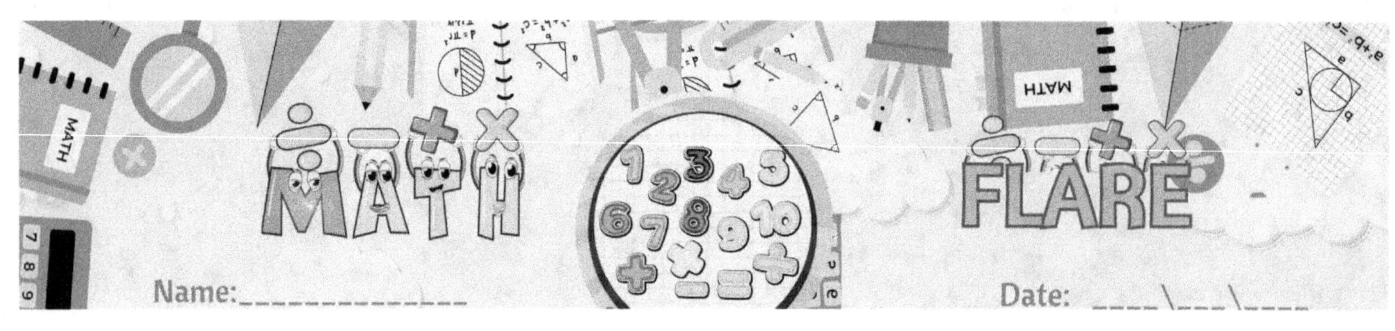

23) $\dfrac{5}{6} \times \dfrac{1}{12} =$ _______________

24) $\dfrac{1}{3} \times \dfrac{2}{3} =$ _______________

25) $\dfrac{1}{4} \times \dfrac{6}{11} =$ _______________

26) $\dfrac{1}{4} \times \dfrac{1}{4} =$ _______________

27) $\dfrac{1}{5} \times \dfrac{1}{3} =$ _______________

28) $\dfrac{10}{11} \times \dfrac{1}{2} =$ _______________

29) $\dfrac{1}{7} \times \dfrac{1}{6} =$ _______________

30) $\dfrac{2}{3} \times \dfrac{8}{9} =$ _______________

31) $\dfrac{1}{5} \times \dfrac{1}{6} =$ _______________

32) $\dfrac{1}{3} \times \dfrac{8}{9} =$ _______________

33) $\dfrac{11}{12} \times \dfrac{1}{2} =$ _______________

34) $\dfrac{1}{4} \times \dfrac{1}{2} =$ _______________

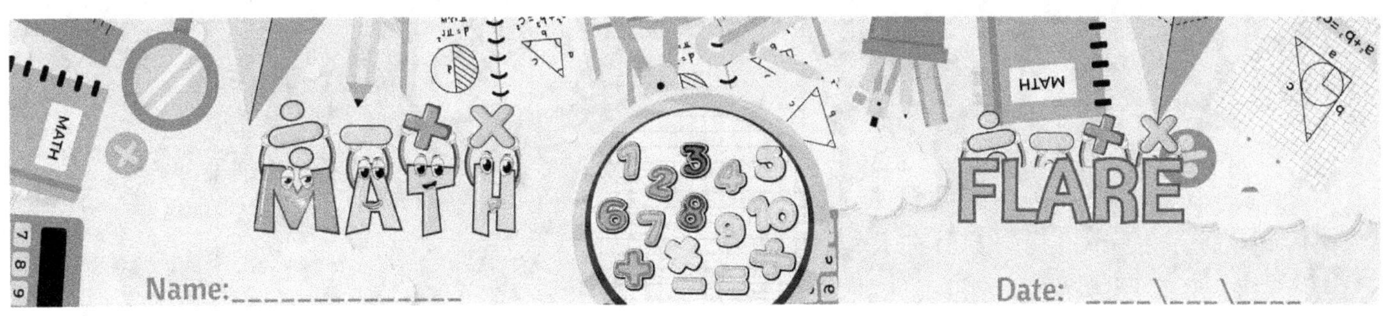

35) $\dfrac{1}{6} \times \dfrac{6}{7} =$ _______________

36) $\dfrac{8}{11} \times \dfrac{2}{3} =$ _______________

37) $\dfrac{4}{5} \times \dfrac{2}{5} =$ _______________

38) $\dfrac{3}{10} \times \dfrac{1}{2} =$ _______________

39) $\dfrac{1}{2} \times \dfrac{1}{4} =$ _______________

40) $\dfrac{5}{8} \times \dfrac{5}{7} =$ _______________

41) $\dfrac{1}{2} \times \dfrac{8}{11} =$ _______________

42) $\dfrac{2}{3} \times \dfrac{2}{3} =$ _______________

43) $\dfrac{3}{10} \times \dfrac{7}{10} =$ _______________

44) $\dfrac{5}{7} \times \dfrac{5}{7} =$ _______________

45) $\dfrac{4}{5} \times \dfrac{3}{4} =$ _______________

46) $\dfrac{1}{4} \times \dfrac{5}{6} =$ _______________

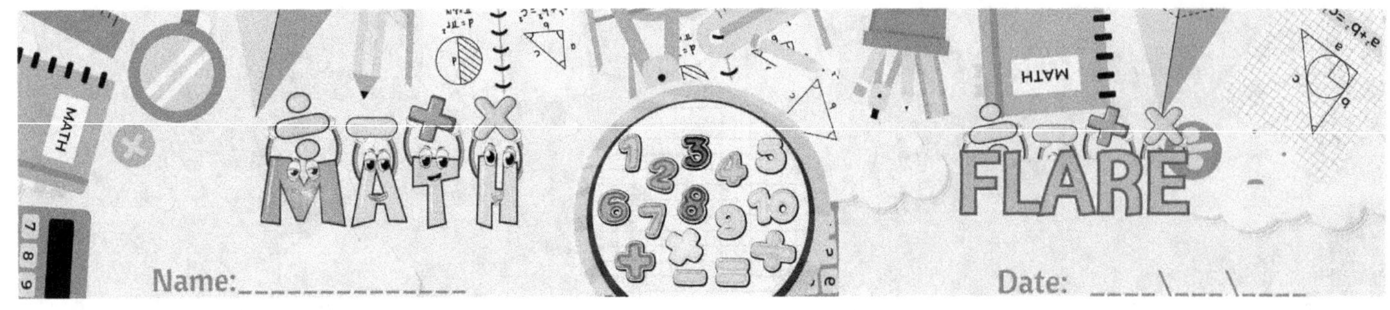

Fractions Division

Find the quotient.

1) $\dfrac{2}{9} \div \dfrac{10}{11} =$ $\dfrac{11}{45}$

$\dfrac{2}{9} \times \dfrac{11}{10} = \dfrac{2 \times 11}{9 \times 10} = \dfrac{22}{90}$

2) $\dfrac{2}{3} \div \dfrac{6}{12} =$

3) $\dfrac{1}{2} \div \dfrac{6}{8} =$

4) $\dfrac{5}{11} \div \dfrac{2}{5} =$

5) $\dfrac{4}{5} \div \dfrac{5}{7} =$

6) $\dfrac{2}{3} \div \dfrac{4}{11} =$

7) $\dfrac{1}{10} \div \dfrac{2}{4} =$

8) $\dfrac{1}{12} \div \dfrac{5}{6} =$

9) $\dfrac{7}{11} \div \dfrac{1}{3} =$

10) $\dfrac{2}{9} \div \dfrac{2}{4} =$

11) $\dfrac{7}{12} \div \dfrac{4}{9} =$ _______________

12) $\dfrac{1}{6} \div \dfrac{1}{12} =$ _______________

13) $\dfrac{1}{8} \div \dfrac{5}{10} =$ _______________

14) $\dfrac{6}{7} \div \dfrac{3}{7} =$ _______________

15) $\dfrac{1}{2} \div \dfrac{4}{5} =$ _______________

16) $\dfrac{3}{5} \div \dfrac{2}{5} =$ _______________

17) $\dfrac{1}{4} \div \dfrac{1}{12} =$ _______________

18) $\dfrac{1}{12} \div \dfrac{2}{6} =$ _______________

19) $\dfrac{2}{9} \div \dfrac{1}{2} =$ _______________

20) $\dfrac{1}{3} \div \dfrac{5}{7} =$ _______________

21) $\dfrac{1}{2} \div \dfrac{2}{7} =$ _______________

22) $\dfrac{10}{11} \div \dfrac{7}{8} =$ _______________

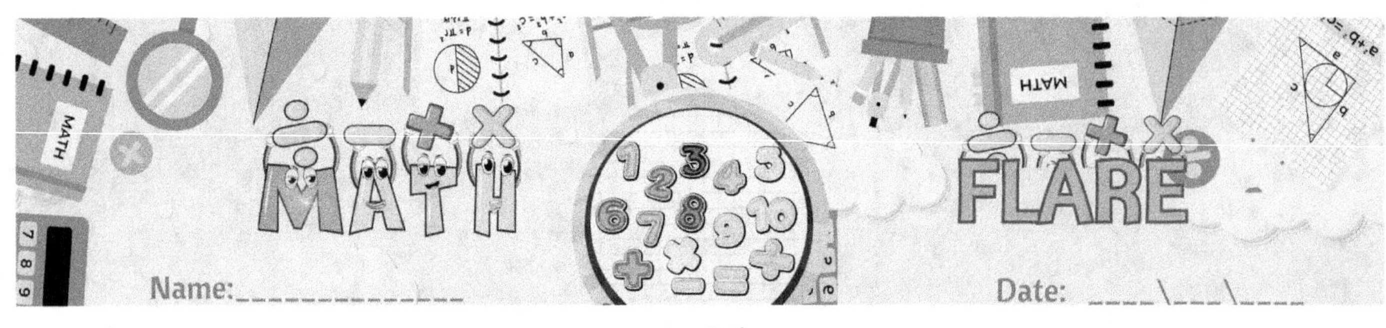

23) $\dfrac{1}{2} \div \dfrac{1}{2} =$ _______________

24) $\dfrac{7}{12} \div \dfrac{3}{12} =$ _______________

25) $\dfrac{3}{4} \div \dfrac{1}{4} =$ _______________

26) $\dfrac{1}{10} \div \dfrac{2}{6} =$ _______________

27) $\dfrac{1}{2} \div \dfrac{9}{11} =$ _______________

28) $\dfrac{5}{12} \div \dfrac{8}{10} =$ _______________

29) $\dfrac{5}{9} \div \dfrac{7}{8} =$ _______________

30) $\dfrac{3}{7} \div \dfrac{1}{3} =$ _______________

31) $\dfrac{4}{5} \div \dfrac{1}{2} =$ _______________

32) $\dfrac{1}{3} \div \dfrac{3}{4} =$ _______________

33) $\dfrac{1}{2} \div \dfrac{2}{6} =$ _______________

34) $\dfrac{5}{8} \div \dfrac{1}{11} =$ _______________

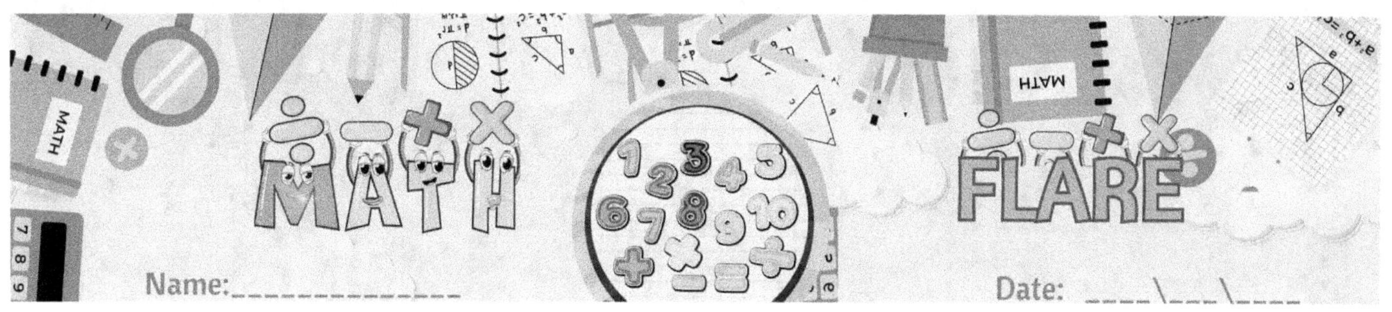

Name:_______________ Date: ___________

35) $\dfrac{1}{4} \div \dfrac{7}{9} =$ _______________

36) $\dfrac{1}{6} \div \dfrac{2}{3} =$ _______________

37) $\dfrac{1}{12} \div \dfrac{1}{2} =$ _______________

38) $\dfrac{3}{11} \div \dfrac{4}{10} =$ _______________

39) $\dfrac{7}{12} \div \dfrac{3}{11} =$ _______________

40) $\dfrac{3}{5} \div \dfrac{1}{2} =$ _______________

41) $\dfrac{3}{4} \div \dfrac{2}{3} =$ _______________

42) $\dfrac{5}{9} \div \dfrac{4}{6} =$ _______________

43) $\dfrac{1}{2} \div \dfrac{6}{12} =$ _______________

44) $\dfrac{1}{6} \div \dfrac{8}{10} =$ _______________

45) $\dfrac{7}{12} \div \dfrac{2}{7} =$ _______________

46) $\dfrac{2}{3} \div \dfrac{3}{9} =$ _______________

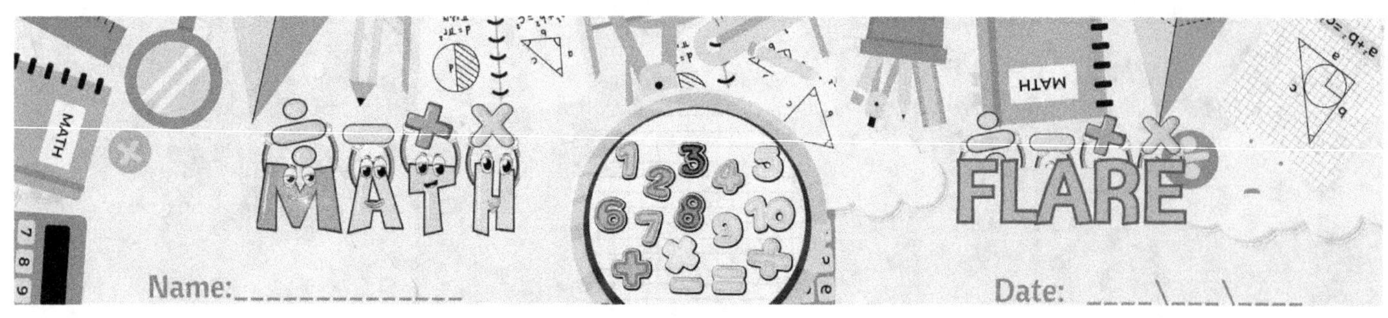

Fractions Addition Word Problems

1) Aria spent $\frac{1}{3}$ of her salary on watches and then $\frac{1}{2}$ of the money on food. How much money did she spend?

$$\frac{1}{3} + \frac{1}{2} = \frac{2\times1 + 3\times1}{3\times2} = \frac{2+3}{6} = \frac{5}{6} \qquad \text{she spent } \frac{5}{6} \text{ of her money}$$

2) Joseph read $\frac{4}{9}$ of his book yesterday and $\frac{4}{10}$ of it today. How much of his book has he read in total?

3) Ariana bought $\frac{2}{7}$ of a pound of ground beef and then added another $\frac{4}{7}$ of a pound to make a hamburger patty. How much ground beef did she use in total?

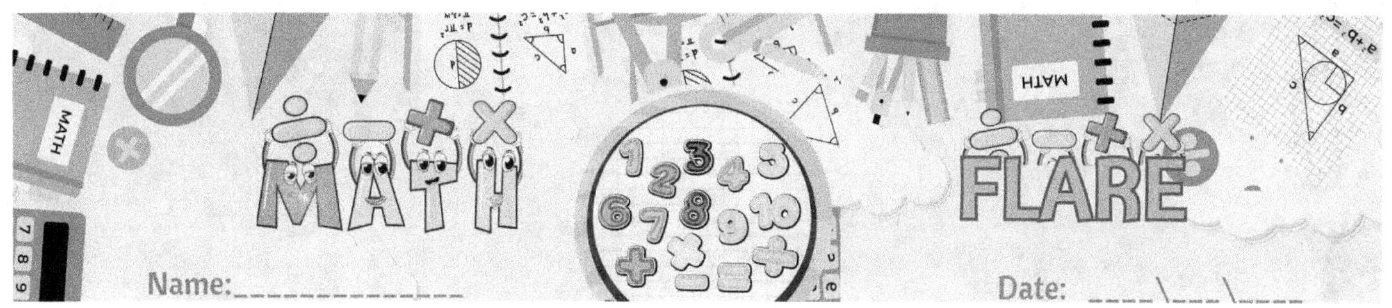

4) Nolan ran $\frac{3}{6}$ of a mile and then walked another $\frac{1}{4}$ of a mile. How far did he travel in total?

5) If the sum of two fractions is $\frac{5}{6}$ and the first fraction is $\frac{1}{3}$, what is the second fraction?

6) Zara used $\frac{2}{5}$ of a pound of coffee and then added another $\frac{1}{6}$ of a pound to make a pot of coffee. How much coffee did she use in total?

7) Sebastian writes $\frac{3}{7}$ of his paper before lunch. After lunch, he writes $\frac{1}{4}$ more. How much of his paper has he finished in total?

8) Hannah used $\frac{4}{10}$ of a stick of butter in a recipe and then used another $\frac{2}{6}$ of the stick in a different recipe. How much of the stick did she use in total?

9) Victoria used $\frac{1}{5}$ of a container of milk in a recipe and then used another $\frac{2}{5}$ of the container in a different recipe. How much of the container did she use in total?

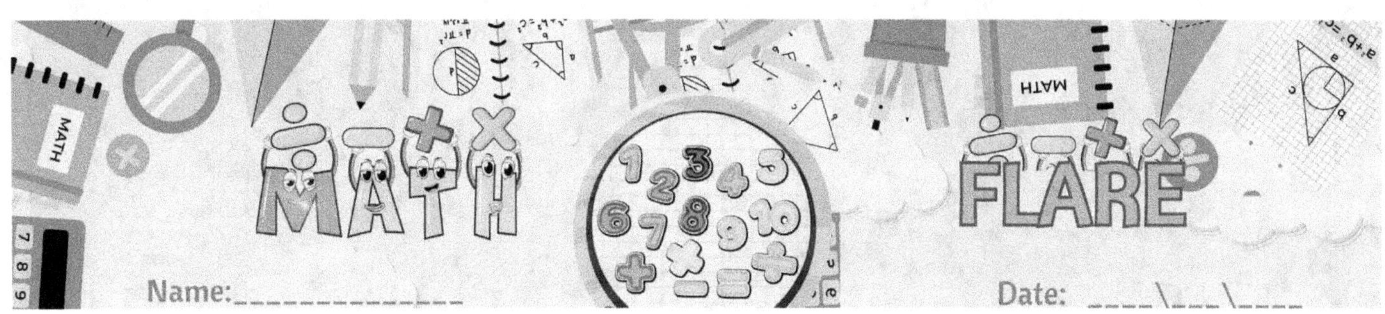

10) A recipe calls for $\frac{1}{6}$ cups of milk and $\frac{7}{9}$ cups of suger. How much of the ingredients are needed in total for the recipe?

11) A recipe calls for $\frac{2}{4}$ cups of peanut butter and $\frac{1}{3}$ cups of jelly. How much of the ingredients are needed in total for the recipe?

12) What is the sum of $\frac{2}{6}$ and $\frac{5}{9}$?

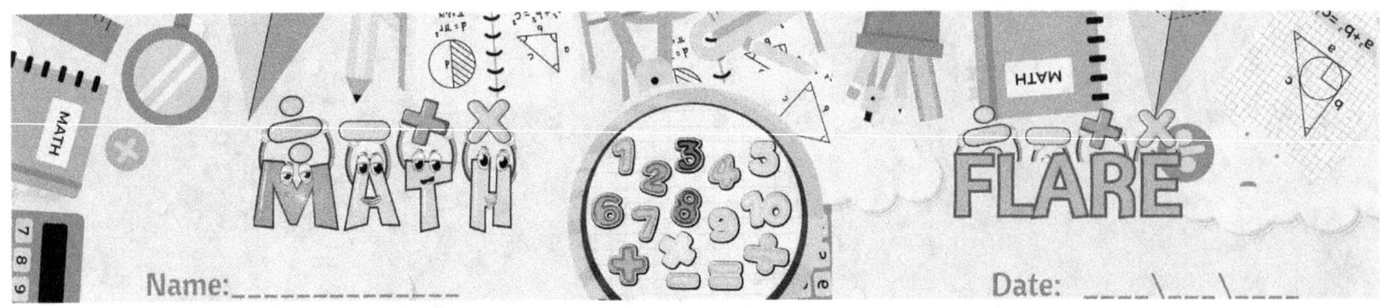

13) Wyatt solved $\frac{1}{3}$ of a math quiz and then $\frac{1}{4}$ of the same quiz. How much of the quiz has she solved?

14) Alexander swam $\frac{1}{9}$ of a lap and then floated another $\frac{4}{5}$ of a lap. How far did he travel in total?

15) A recipe calls for $\frac{1}{2}$ cups of flour and $\frac{1}{2}$ cups of sugar. How much dry ingredient in total is needed for the recipe?

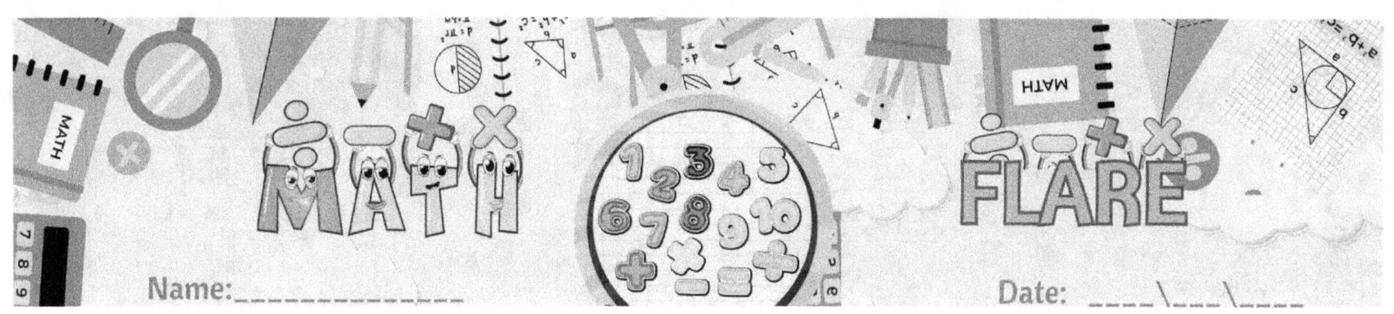

16) Dominic walked $\frac{3}{6}$ of a mile and then run another $\frac{1}{3}$ of a mile. How far did he travel in total?

17) Aiden drank $\frac{4}{7}$ of a bottle of water and then drank another $\frac{2}{6}$ of the bottle later. How much of the bottle did he drink in total?

18) Leah read $\frac{1}{3}$ pages of her book before bed. She then read another $\frac{1}{5}$ pages before falling asleep. How much of her book did she read in total?

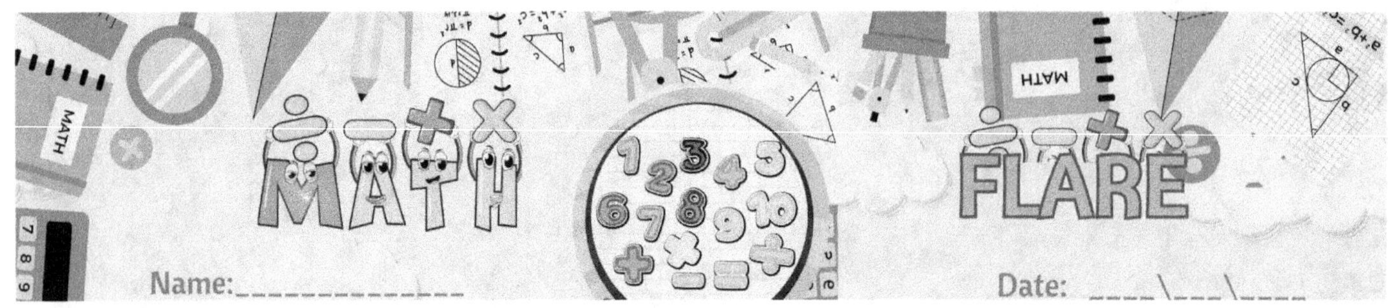

19) A recipe calls for $\frac{3}{9}$ cups of milk and $\frac{2}{7}$ cups of butter. How much of the ingredients are needed in total?

20) A recipe calls for $\frac{2}{5}$ cups of strawberries and $\frac{2}{6}$ cups of bananas. How much fruit is needed in total for the recipe?

21) Hazel cycled $\frac{5}{10}$ miles. She then stopped to buy some groceries. Then she cycled $\frac{2}{7}$ more miles. How far did Hazel cycle in total?

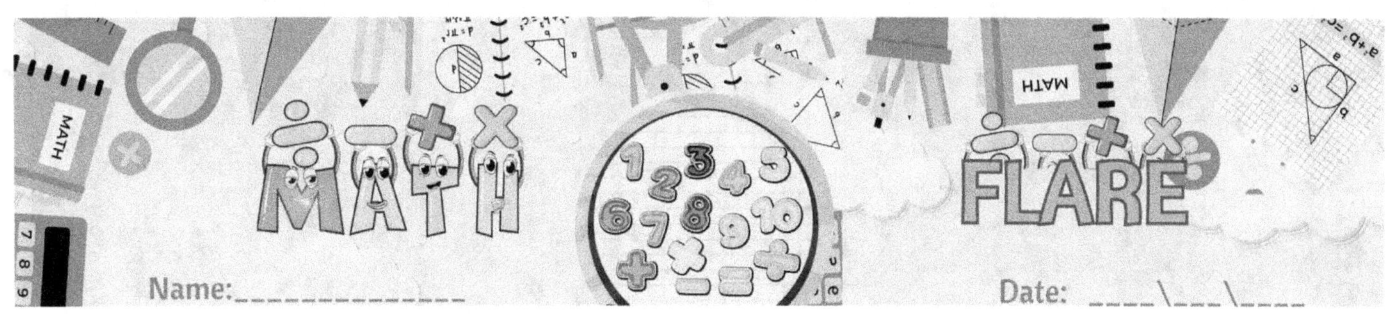

22) Sebastian drove $\frac{1}{3}$ of a mile and then walked $\frac{1}{3}$ of a mile to his friend's house. How far did he travel in total?

23) Molly finished $\frac{2}{8}$ of a book and then read $\frac{5}{10}$ of the remaining pages. How much of the book has she read?

24) Madison baked $\frac{1}{5}$ of her cakes for her friends and then kept $\frac{2}{8}$ of them for herself. How many cakes did she bake in total?

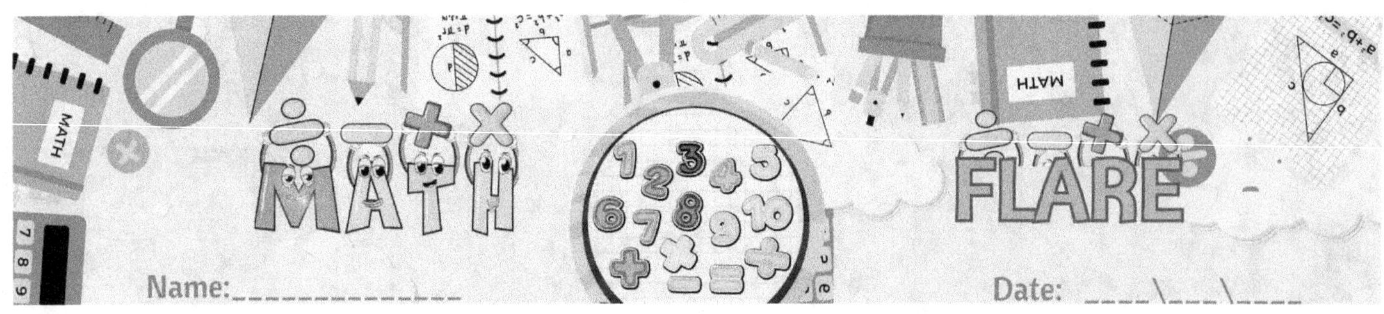

25) Liam ate $\frac{6}{10}$ of a pizza for lunch and then ate another $\frac{1}{10}$ of the pizza for dinner. How much of the pizza did he eat in total?

26) Evan practiced math for $\frac{1}{3}$ of an hour and then played video games for another $\frac{1}{2}$ of an hour. How much time did he spend on these activities in total?

27) Maria made a salad with $\frac{2}{7}$ of a cup of lettuce and $\frac{2}{5}$ of a cup of spinach. How much salad did she make in total?

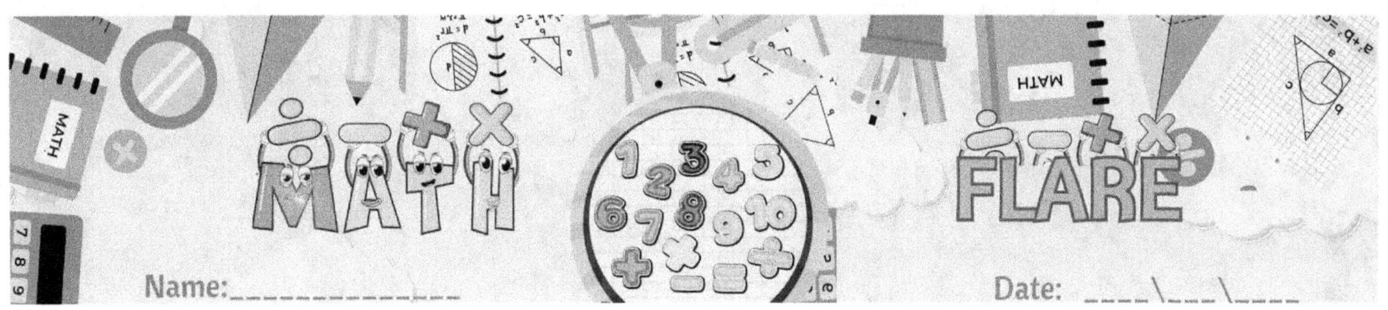

28) A recipe calls for $\frac{4}{9}$ cups of milk and $\frac{1}{3}$ cups of cream. How much liquid in total is needed for the recipe?

29) Natalia used $\frac{5}{8}$ of a cup of flour and then $\frac{2}{7}$ of a cup of sugar in her baking. How much of the ingredients did she use in total?

30) A juice recipe calls for $\frac{5}{8}$ cups of orange juice and $\frac{2}{6}$ cups of apple juice. How much juice is needed in total for the recipe?

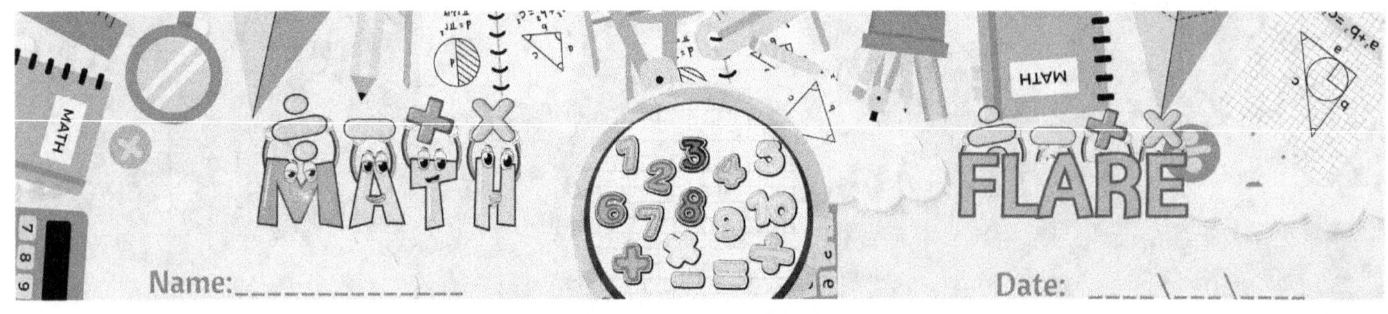

Fractions Subtraction Word Problems

1) A container has $\frac{2}{5}$ of a gallon of milk. If $\frac{2}{6}$ of the milk is taken out and put into another container, how much milk is left in the original container in gallons?

$$\frac{2}{5} - \frac{2}{6} = \frac{2\times6 + 2\times5}{5\times6} = \frac{12 - 10}{30} = \frac{2}{30} = \frac{1}{15}$$

there is $\frac{1}{15}$ gallons of milk left in original container.

2) Kinsley wants to make a dish that calls for $\frac{2}{9}$ of a cup of yogurt. She only has $\frac{1}{9}$ of a cup of yogurt left. How much more yogurt does she need to make the dish?

3) Grayson has $\frac{2}{3}$ of a liter of water. He drinks $\frac{1}{4}$ of the water. How much water is left in liters?

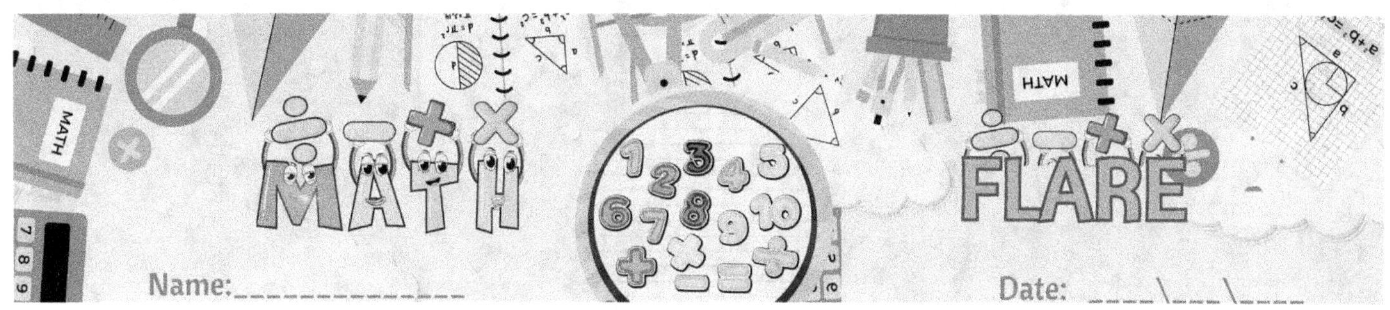

4) Hunter has a rope that is $\frac{5}{10}$ of a meter long. If he cuts off $\frac{3}{8}$ of the rope, how long is the remaining rope in meters?

5) Lillian has $\frac{5}{9}$ of a container of Calculators. She gives $\frac{1}{2}$ of the Calculators to her sister. How much Calculators does she have left?

6) A recipe calls for $\frac{2}{3}$ of a cup of sugar. If $\frac{2}{8}$ of the sugar is already used, how much sugar is left in cups?

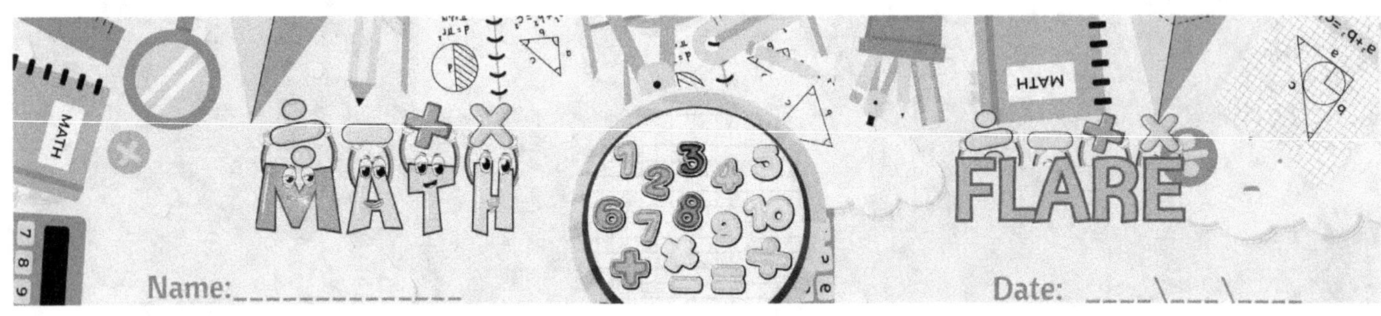

7) Harper is knitting a scarf that needs $\frac{1}{2}$ of the yarn. If she has already used $\frac{6}{9}$ yards of yarn, how much does she have left?

8) Daniel has $\frac{8}{10}$ of a liter of juice. He drinks $\frac{1}{7}$ of the juice. How much juice is left in liters?

9) Natalie is making a sweet dish and needs $\frac{4}{5}$ of a cup of strawberries. She has already used $\frac{6}{8}$ of a cup. How much more strawberry does she need?

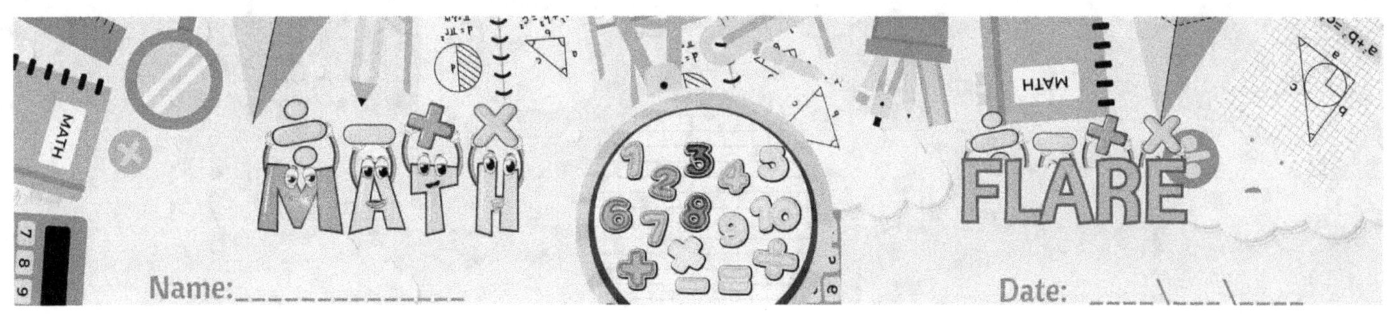

Name:_________________ Date: _______________

10) Brooklyn has $\frac{1}{2}$ of a pound of flour. She uses $\frac{1}{5}$ of the flour to make a pencake. How much flour is left in pounds?

11) Savannah has $\frac{5}{6}$ of a pound of beef. She cooks $\frac{3}{8}$ of the beef. How much beef is left in pounds?

12) Xavier has $\frac{1}{2}$ of a bag of apples. He takes out $\frac{1}{6}$ of the apples. How many apples are in the bag now?

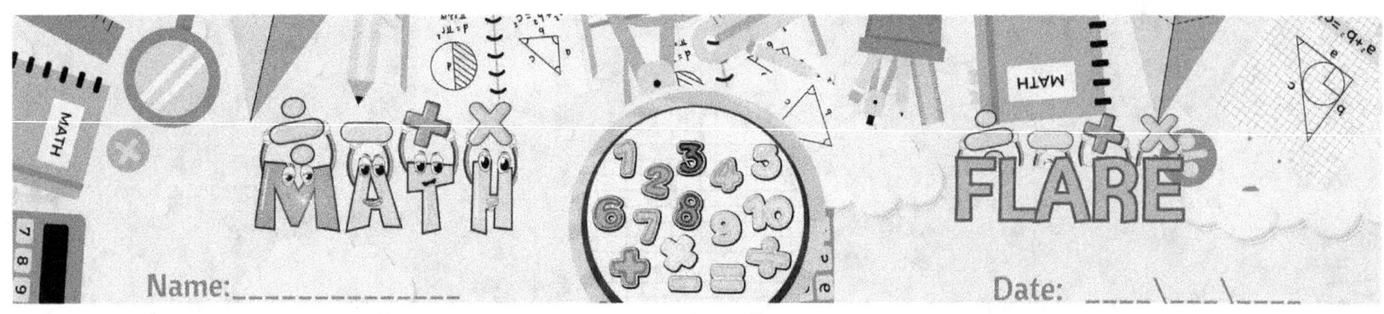

13) Raelynn had $\frac{8}{9}$ of a cup of milk. If $\frac{3}{8}$ of the milk is spilled, how much milk is left in cups?

14) Brielle is running on a track that is $\frac{1}{2}$ of a mile long. She has already run $\frac{2}{7}$ of the mile. How much further does she have to run?

15) Valentina needs $\frac{6}{7}$ of a pound of cheese to make pizza. She only has $\frac{1}{2}$ of a pound of cheese. How much more cheese does she need to buy?

16) Victoria bought $\frac{7}{10}$ of a pound of peanuts. After sharing $\frac{2}{5}$ of the peanuts with her friend, how many pounds of peanuts did Victoria have left?

17) Levi has $\frac{5}{6}$ of a pizza left over from last night. He eats $\frac{7}{10}$ of the pizza for lunch. How much pizza does he have left?

18) Vincent has a collection of Crayons that weighs $\frac{4}{6}$ of a pound. If he loses $\frac{1}{6}$ of the weight, how much does the collection now weigh in pounds?

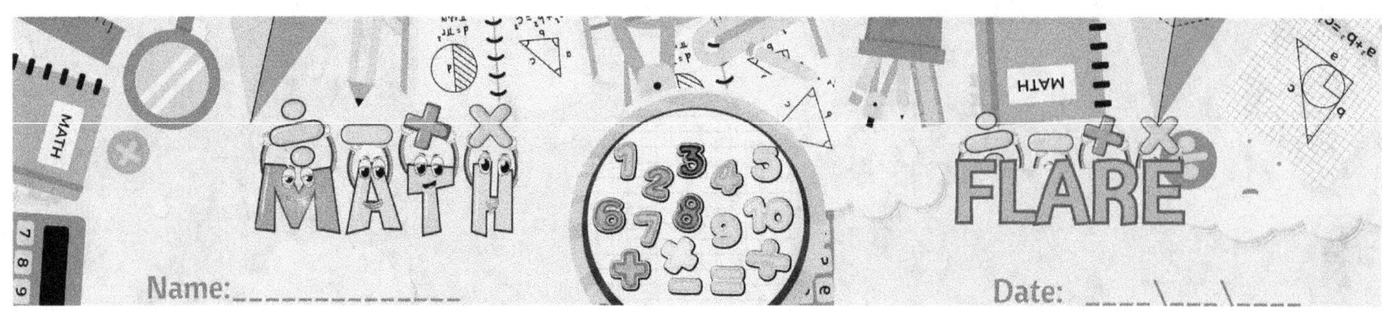

19) A recipe calls for $\frac{4}{5}$ of a cup of milk. If $\frac{4}{8}$ of the milk is already used, how much milk is left in cups?

20) Mila has $\frac{6}{7}$ of a pound of ground chicken. She uses $\frac{3}{7}$ of the chicken to make a burger. How much chicken is left in pounds?

21) Zoey has a book that is $\frac{1}{2}$ of an inch thick. She reads $\frac{1}{3}$ of the book. How thick is the remaining portion of the book in inches?

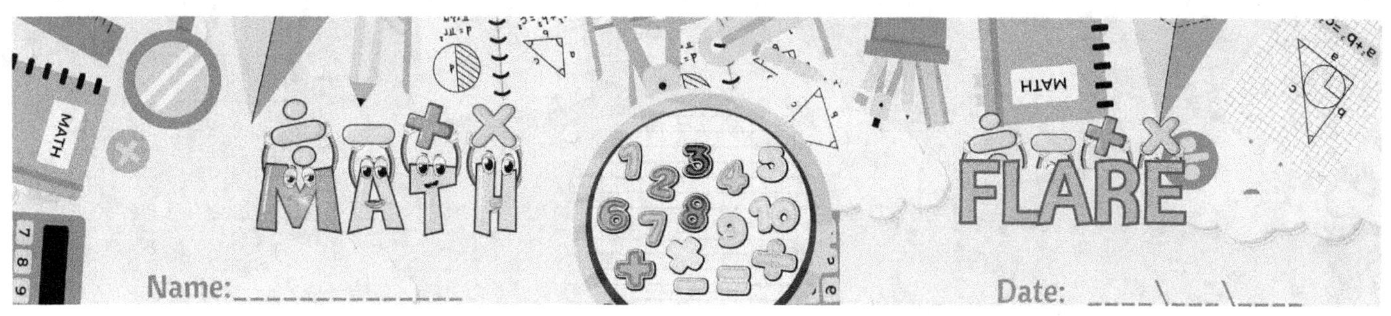

22) Tristan and Emilia are cooking dinner and need $\frac{7}{8}$ of a cup of oil. Tristan accidentally spills $\frac{3}{10}$ of a cup of oil. How much oil do they have left?

23) Kingston has a rope that is $\frac{5}{6}$ of a foot long. He cuts $\frac{3}{7}$ of the rope. How long is the remaining rope in feet?

24) Levi is making a sandwich that calls for $\frac{7}{8}$ of a pound of beef. He only has $\frac{3}{6}$ of a pound of beef left. How much more beef does he need to make the sandwich?

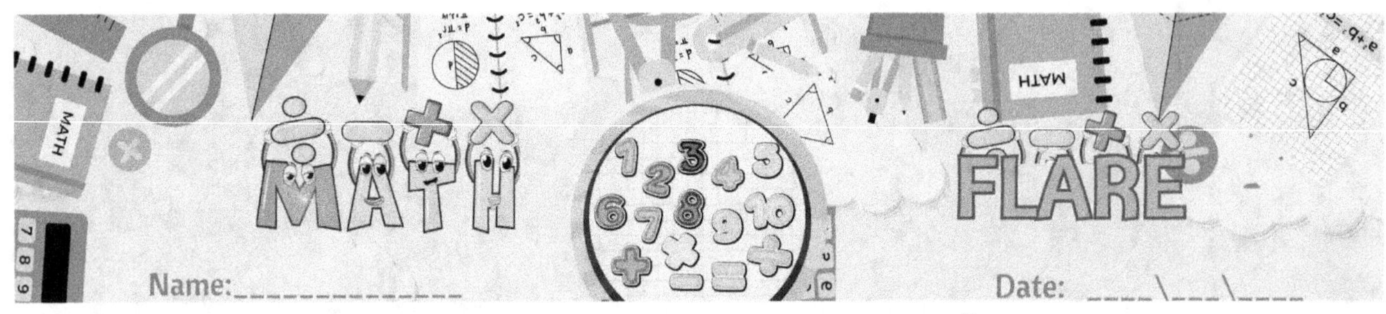

25) Elizabeth bought a bag of flour that weighed $\frac{5}{10}$ pounds. She used $\frac{1}{10}$ of the flour to make pencakes. How much flour was left in the bag?

26) Bella needs $\frac{2}{3}$ of a cup of sugar to make lemonade. She only has $\frac{2}{4}$ of a cup of sugar. How much more sugar does she need to make the lemonade?

27) Brandon has a rope that is $\frac{3}{4}$ of a yard long. He cuts off $\frac{2}{3}$ of the rope. How long is the remaining rope in yards?

28) Hailey had a cake that weighed $\frac{8}{9}$ of a pound. She cut off $\frac{2}{8}$ of a pound to share with her friends. How much cake does she have left?

29) Lucas has a length of ribbon that is $\frac{8}{10}$ meters long. He wants to cut off $\frac{4}{10}$ of the ribbon to use for a gift. How long will the remaining ribbon be?

30) Ryan has a rope that is $\frac{2}{3}$ of a meter long. He needs to cut off $\frac{3}{8}$ of a meter to tie a knot. How long is the rope after the knot is tied?

Chapter. 04

Geometry

Area and Perimeter

The area of a shape represents the amount of space it occupies. The perimeter of a shape is the total distance around its outer edge.

Area of Rectangle

For a square, since all four sides are equal, we only need to know the length of one side to find its area. We can calculate the area of a square by multiplying the length of one side by itself (squared). So, if the length of one side of the square is 's', then the area (A) is given by:

$$A = s \times s$$

4 in

4 in

$$A = 4 \times 4$$

$$A = 16$$

Perimeter of Rectangle

For a square, since all four sides are equal, we can find the perimeter by adding up the lengths of all four sides. If 's' represents the length of one side, then the perimeter (P) is given by:

$$P = 4 \times s$$

$$P = 4 \times 4$$

$$P = 16$$

Area of Triangle:

The area of a triangle represents the amount of space enclosed within its three sides. The formula for calculating the area of a triangle depends on the type of triangle. For a general triangle, we use the formula:

$$A = \frac{1}{2} \times base \times height$$

Where:

- *A* represents the area of the triangle.

- The base is the length of any one side of the triangle.

- The height is the perpendicular distance from the base to the opposite vertex.

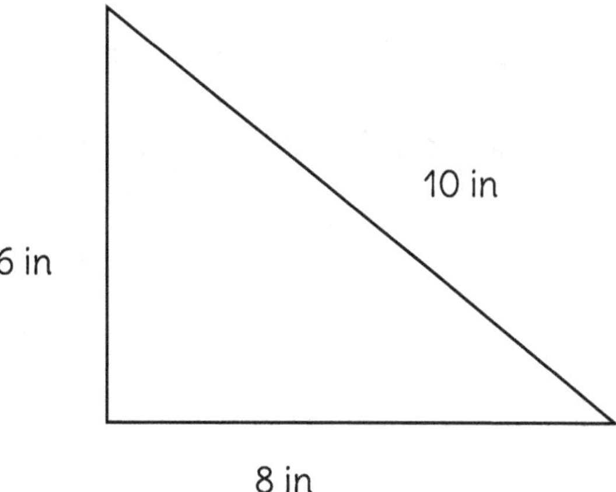

MathFlare - Math Workbook 4th and 5th Grade

$$A = \frac{1}{2} \times \text{base} \times \text{height}$$

$$A = \frac{1}{2} \times 6 \times 8$$

$$A = \frac{1}{2} \times 48$$

$$A = 24$$

Perimeter of Triangle:

The perimeter of a triangle is the total length of its three sides. To find the perimeter, we simply add the lengths of all three sides together:

$$P = \text{side1} + \text{side2} + \text{side3}$$

$$P = 6 + 8 + 10$$

$$P = 24$$

Equilateral Triangle

An equilateral triangle is a triangle in which all three sides are equal in length. To find the area and perimeter of an equilateral triangle, we can use the following formulas:

- Area (A): $\frac{\sqrt{3}}{4} \times a^2$ where a is the length of one side of the equilateral triangle.

- Perimeter (P): $P = 3a$ where a is the length of one side of the equilateral triangle.

Let's solve a problem:

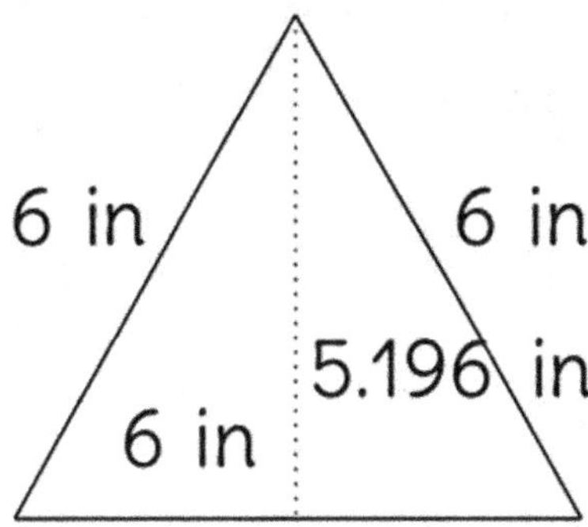

Area of Equilateral Triangle:

$$\text{Area (A): } \frac{\sqrt{3}}{4} \times (6)^2$$

$$\text{Area (A): } \frac{\sqrt{3}}{4} \times 36$$

$$\text{Area (A): } \frac{36\sqrt{3}}{4}$$

$$\text{Area (A): } \frac{36(1.73)}{4}$$

$$\text{Area (A): } \frac{62.35}{4}$$

$$\text{Area (A): } 15.59 \text{ in}^2$$

Perimeter of Equilateral Triangle:

$$P = 3a$$

$$P = 3(6) = 18$$

MathFlare - Math Workbook 4th and 5th Grade

<u>Isosceles Triangle</u>

An isosceles triangle is a triangle with at least two sides of equal length. The angles opposite the equal sides are also equal.

Area of Isosceles Triangle

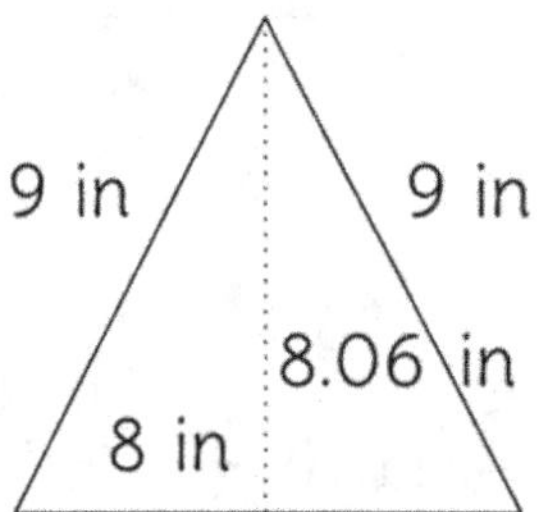

$$A = \frac{1}{2} \times base \times height$$

$$A = \frac{1}{2} \times 8 \times 8$$

$$A = \frac{1}{2} \times 64$$

$$A = 32$$

Perimeter of Isosceles Triangle

The perimeter of a triangle is the total length of its three sides. To find the perimeter, we simply add the lengths of all three sides together:

$$P = side1 + side2 + side3$$

$$P = 9 + 9 + 8$$

$$P = 26$$

Area and Circumference of circles

To find the area (A) and circumference (C) of a circle, we use the following formulas:

1. Area of a Circle (A) = $\pi \times (radius)^2$

    - where π (pi) is a constant with value of (3.14). It is a ratio of the circumference of a circle to its diameter,

    - the radius (r) is the distance from the center of the circle.

2. Circumference of a Circle (C) = $2 \times \pi \times radius$

Let's solve an example: suppose a swimming pool has a radius of 11 meters, we are required to calculate its Area and Circumference:

$$\text{Area } (A) = \pi \times (radius)^2$$

$$A = 3.14 \times 11^2$$

$$A = 3.14 \times 121$$

$$A = 379.94 \text{ square meters}$$

$$\text{Circumference } (C) = 2 \times \pi \times radius$$

$$C = 2 \times 3.14 \times 11$$

$$C = 69.08 \text{ square meters}$$

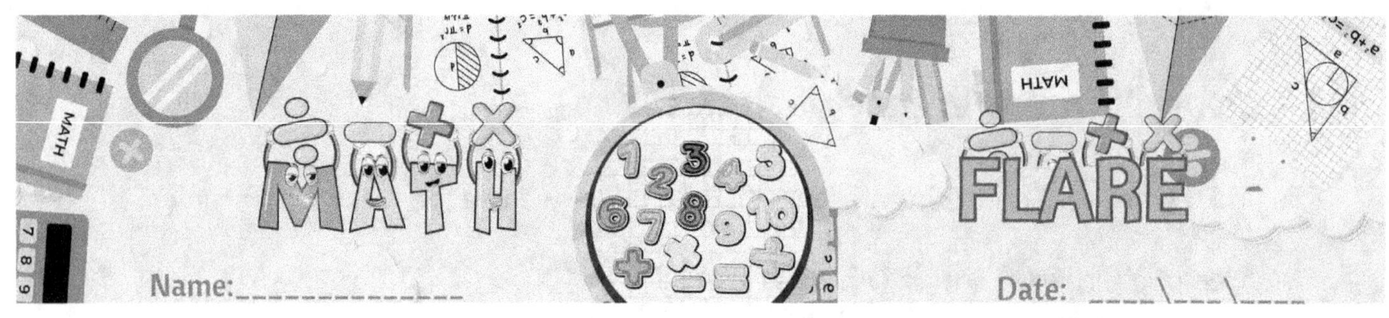

Area and Perimeter: Rectangles and Triangles

1)

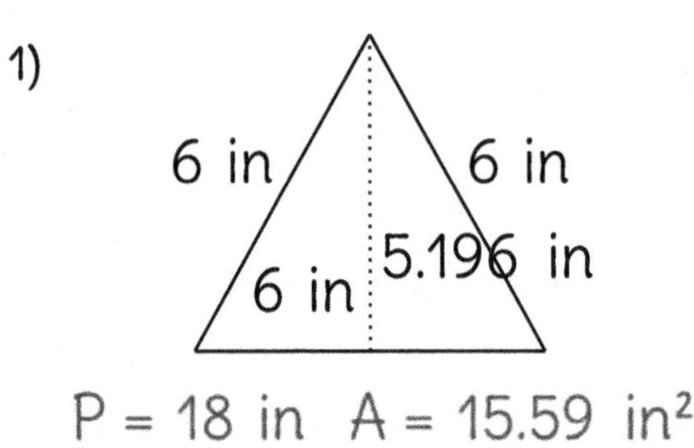

P = 18 in   A = 15.59 in²

2)

P = 32 in   A = 60 in²

3)

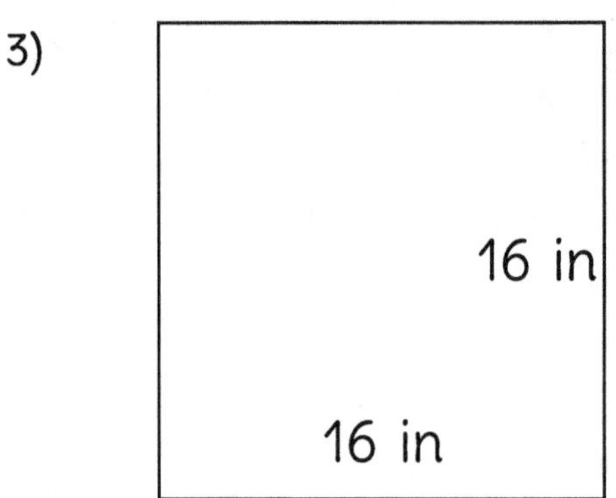

4)

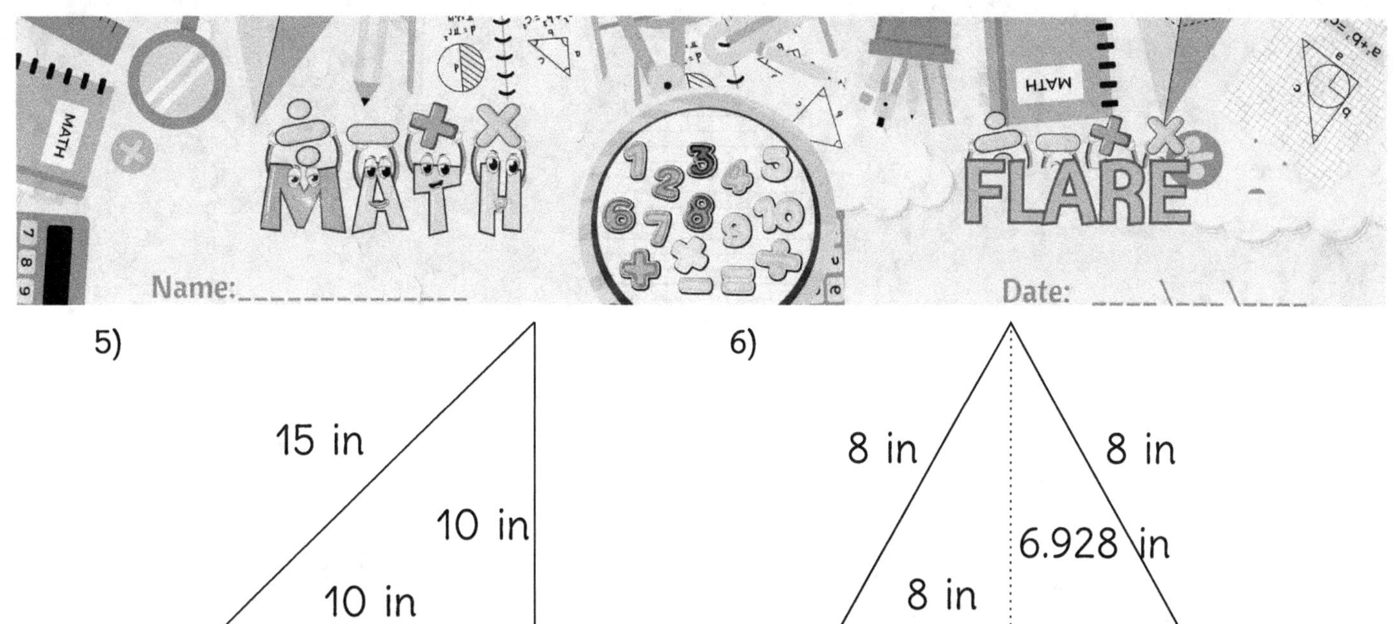

5)

15 in
10 in
10 in

6)

8 in
8 in
8 in
6.928 in

7)

15 in
15 in
13.75 in
12 in

8)

MATH
FLARE
Name:________________
Date: ____________

9)

20 in
15 in
14 in

10)

16 in
16 in
13.856 in
16 in

11)

11 in
8 in
9 in

12)

8 in
8 in
6.928 in
8 in

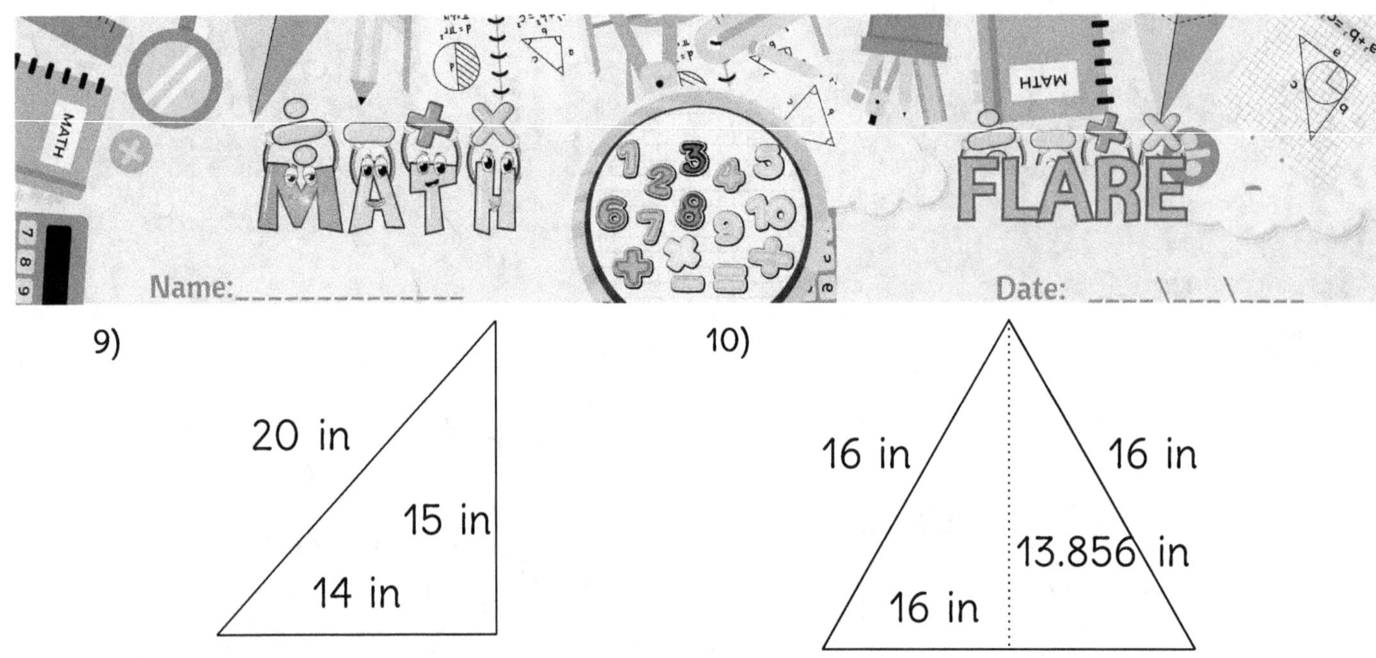

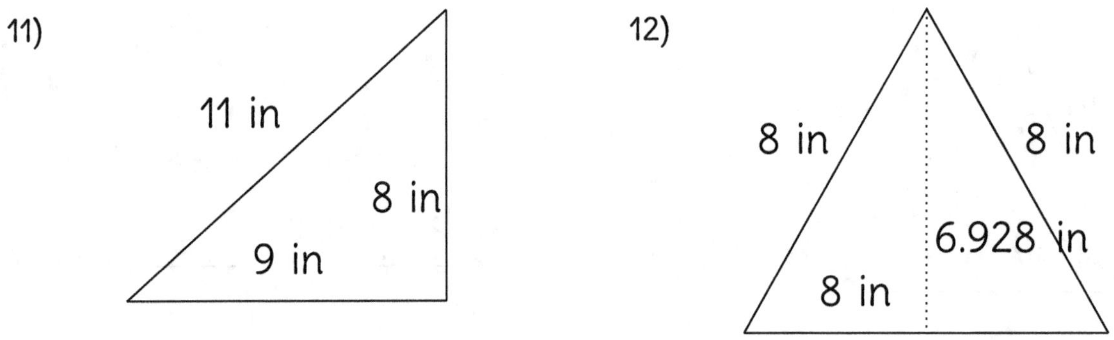

135

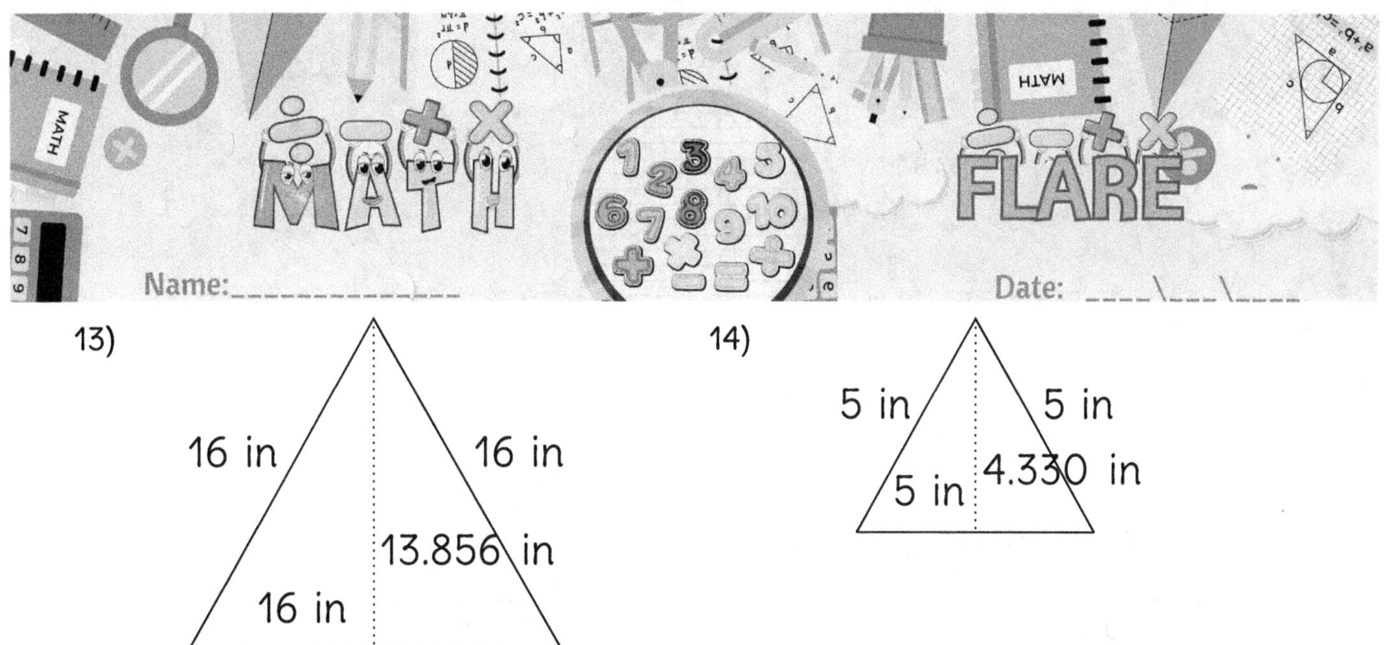

13)

16 in   16 in

13.856 in

16 in

14)

5 in   5 in

5 in   4.330 in

15)

9 in

11 in

16)

10 in   10 in

9.17 in

8 in

Name:
Date:

17)

8 in
8 in
7.42 in
6 in

18)

18 in
12 in
13 in

19)

12 in
12 in
11.12 in
9 in

20)

19 in
13 in
14 in

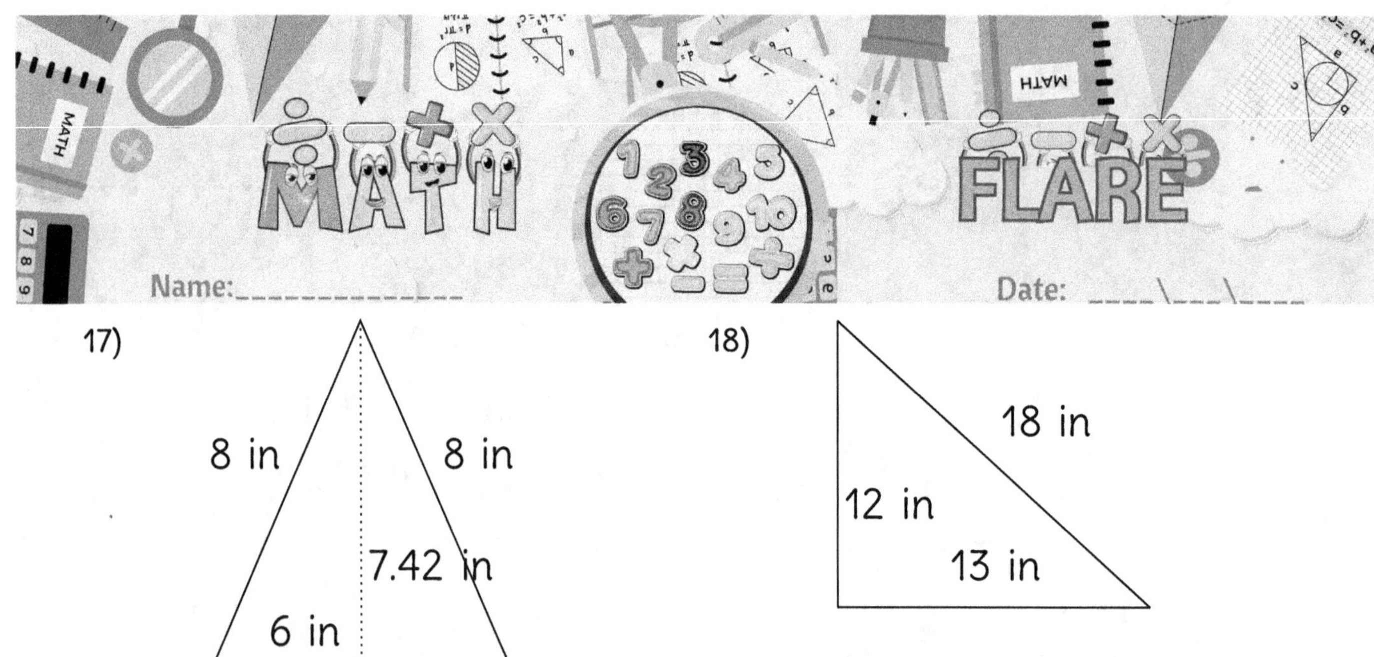

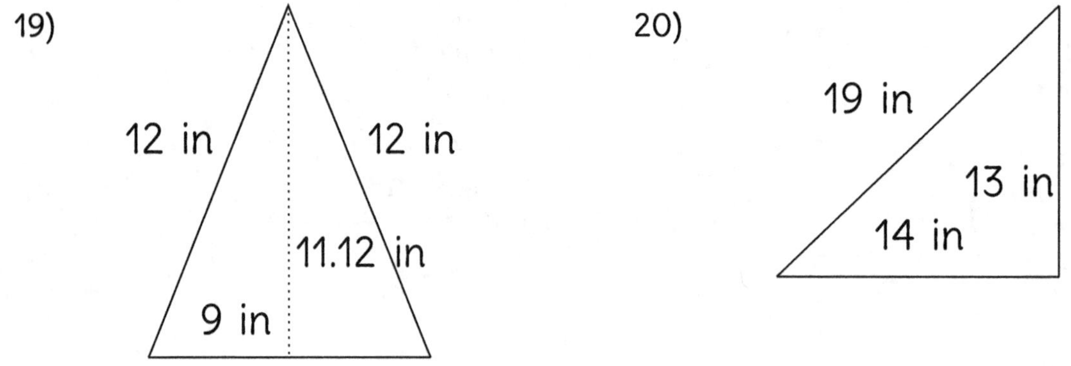

Name:
Date:

21)

17 in
11 in
13 in

22)

17 in
17 in
14.72 in
17 in

23)

14 in
10 in
10 in

24)

7 in
7 in
6.062 in
7 in

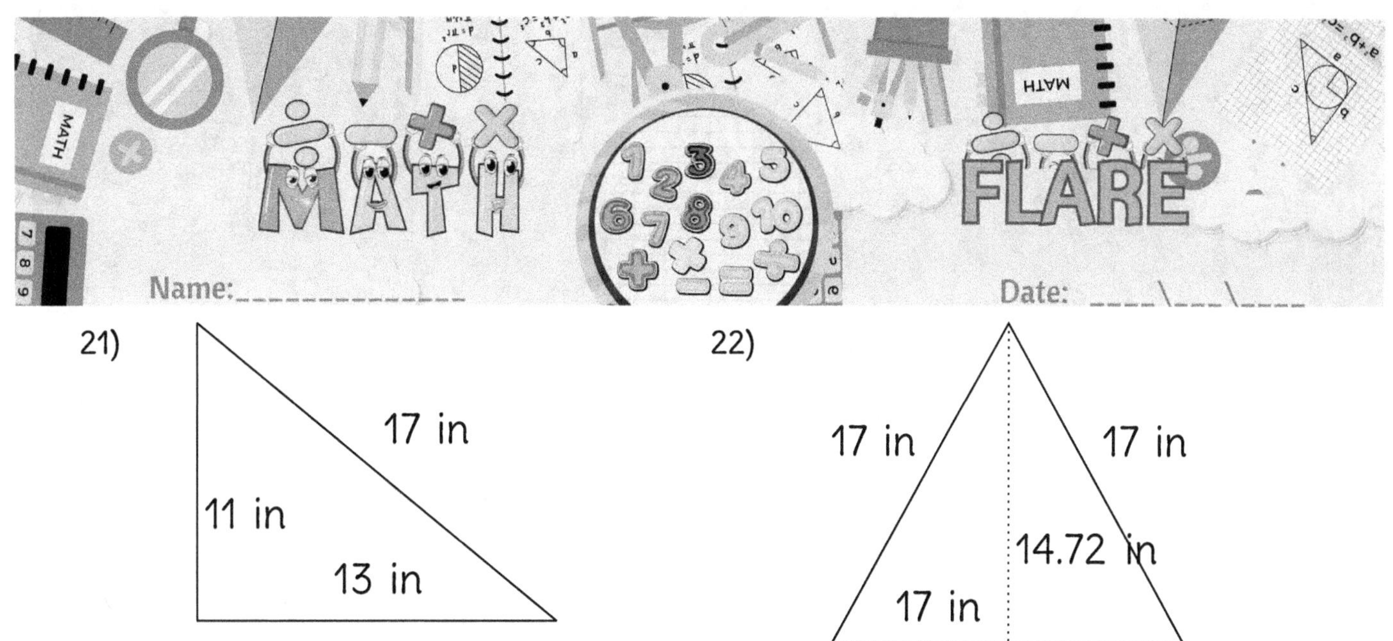

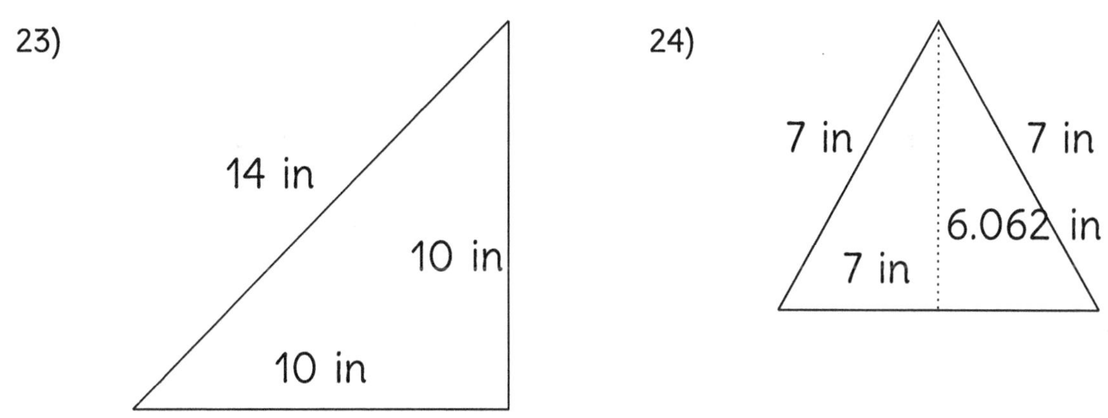

Name:
Date:

25)

18 in
14 in
12 in

26)

19 in
12 in
15 in

27)

16 in
12 in
11 in

28)

20 in
13 in
15 in

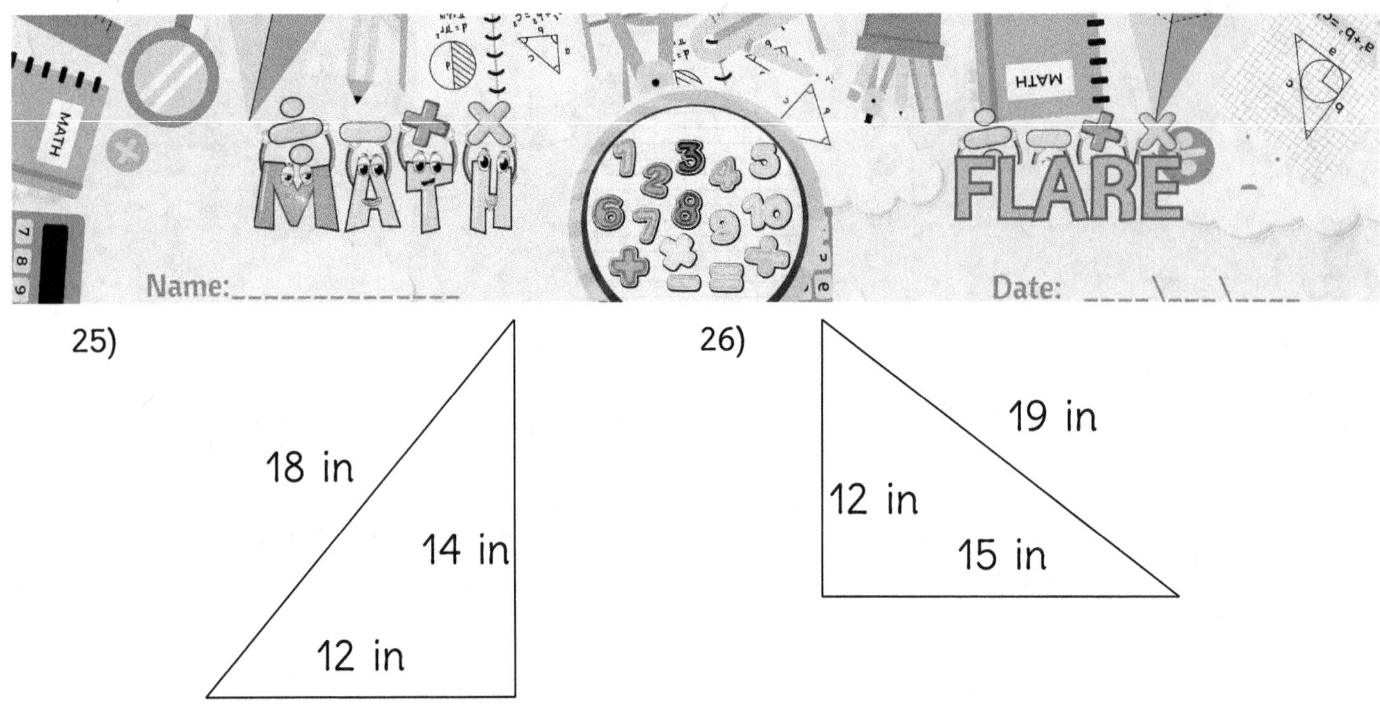

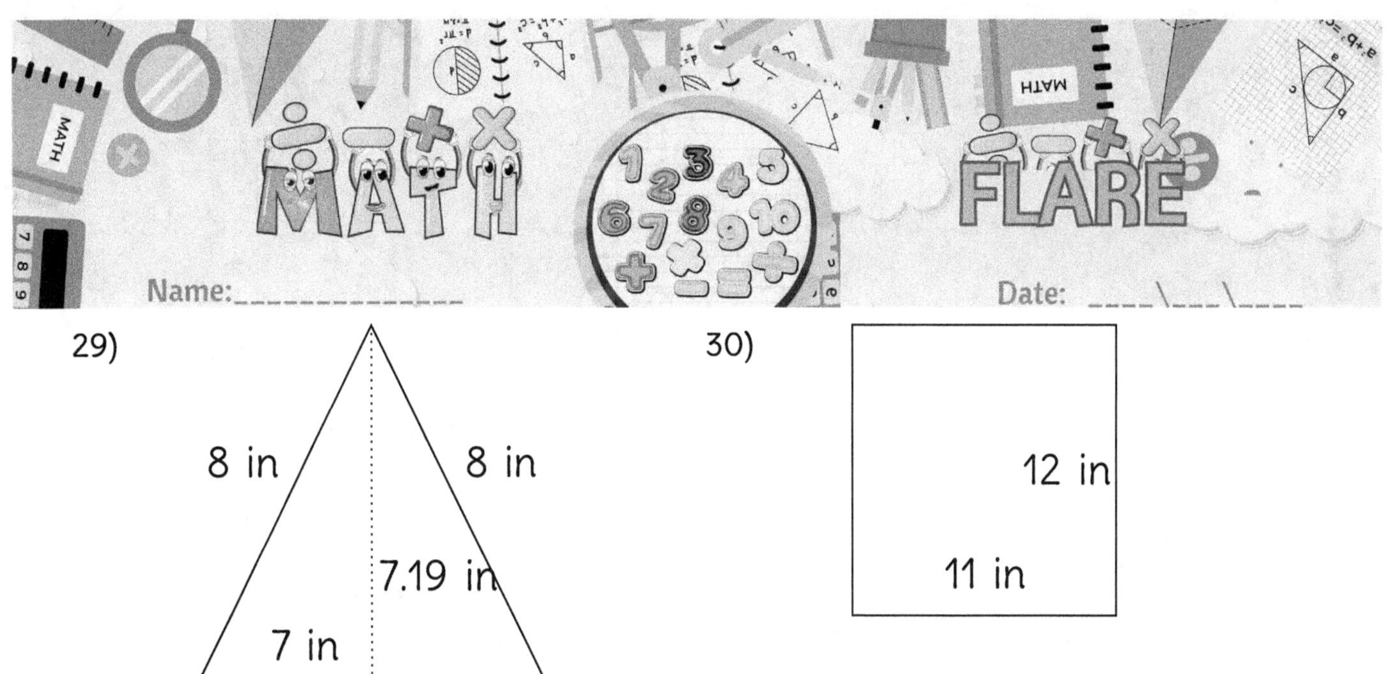

29)

8 in 8 in

7.19 in

7 in

30)

12 in

11 in

31)

8 in

8 in

32)

9 in

10 in

MATH
FLARE
Name:
Date:

33)

20 in
15 in
13 in

34)

23 in
15 in
17 in

35)

6 in
6 in
5.196 in
6 in

36)

11 in
11 in
10.04 in
9 in

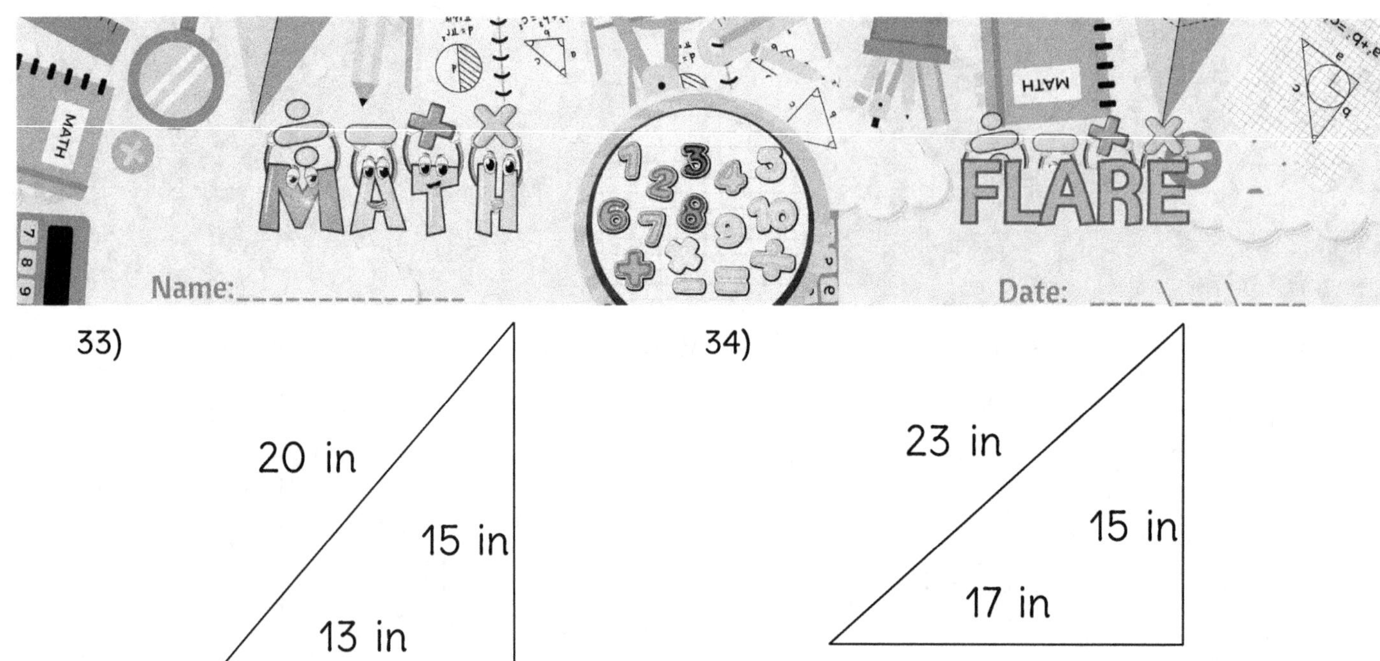

MATH
FLARE
MATH
Name:
Date:

37)

20 in
13 in
15 in

38)

9 in
8 in
5 in

39)

12 in
8 in
10 in

40)

16 in
16 in
13.856 in
16 in

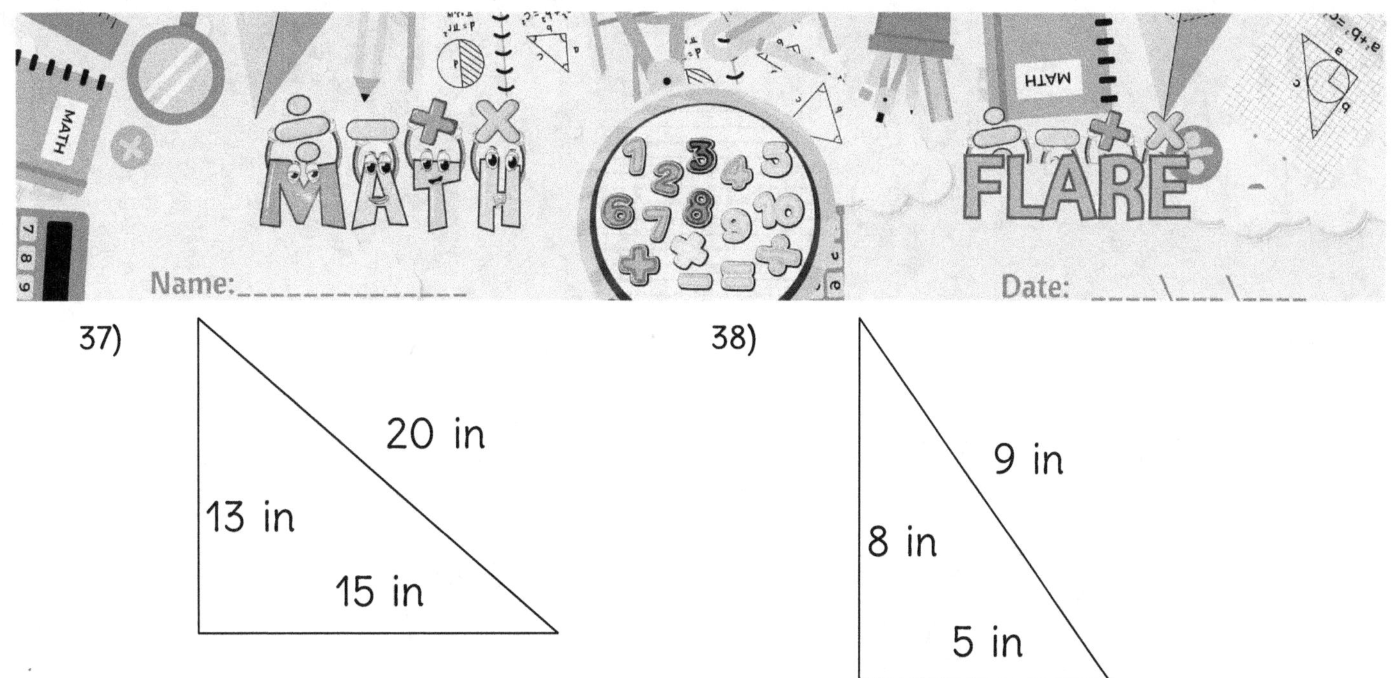

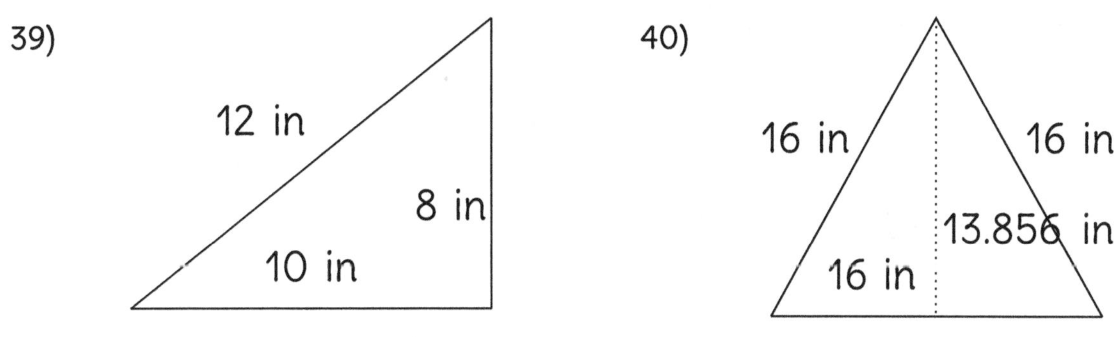

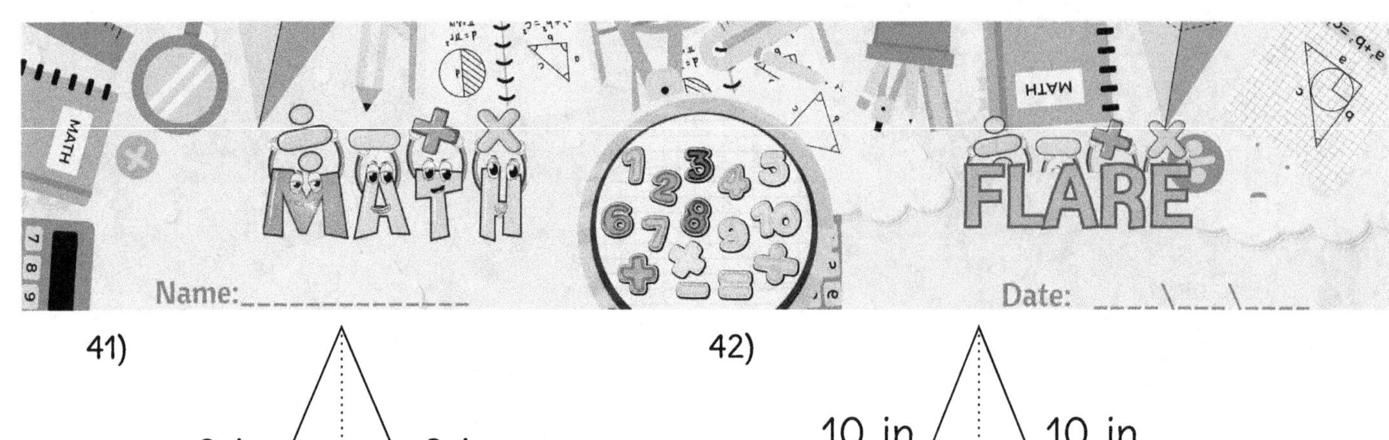

41)

8 in   8 in

7.42 in

6 in

42)

10 in   10 in

9.17 in

8 in

43)

10 in

8 in

44)

14 in

12 in

8 in

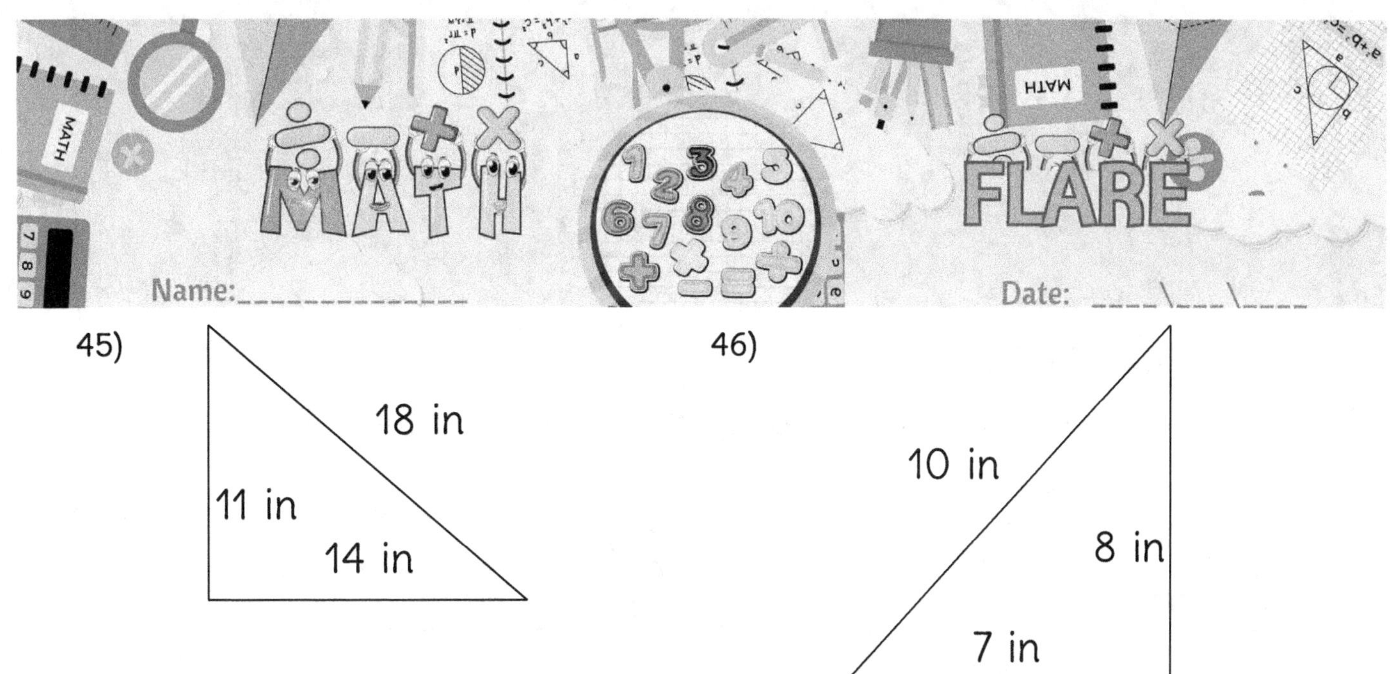

45)

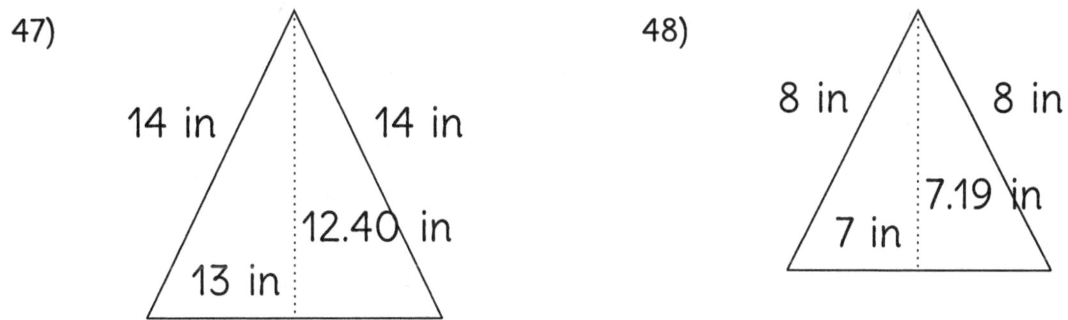

18 in

11 in

14 in

46)

10 in

8 in

7 in

47)

14 in   14 in

12.40 in

13 in

48)

8 in   8 in

7.19 in

7 in

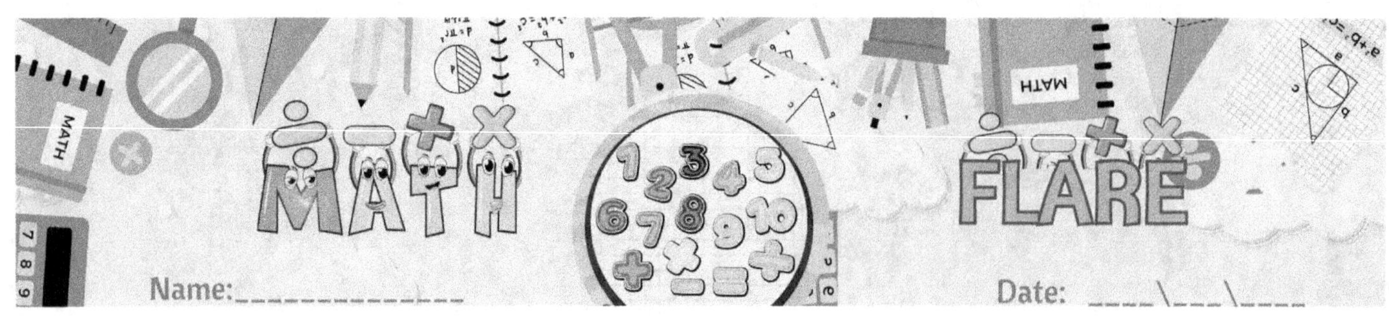

Circumference

Calculate the circumference of each circle. Pi Value = 3.14

1)

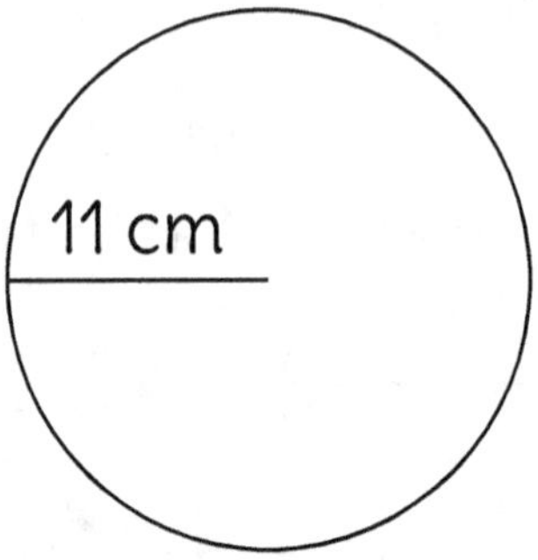

11 cm

C=69.08 cm

2)

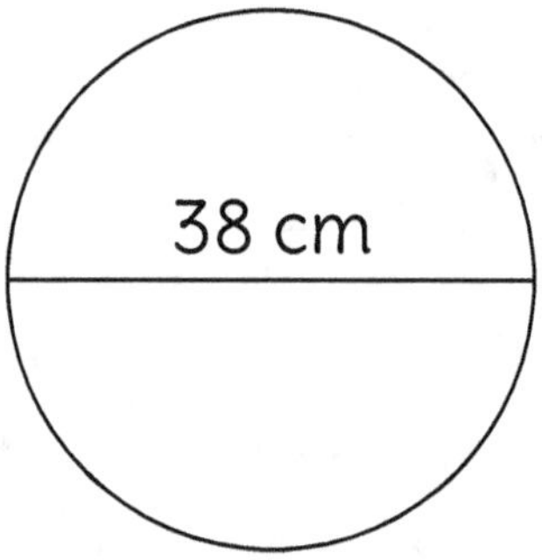

38 cm

____

3)

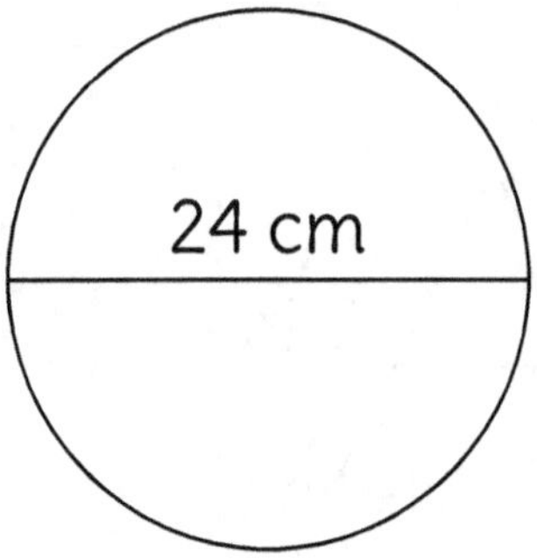

24 cm

____

4)

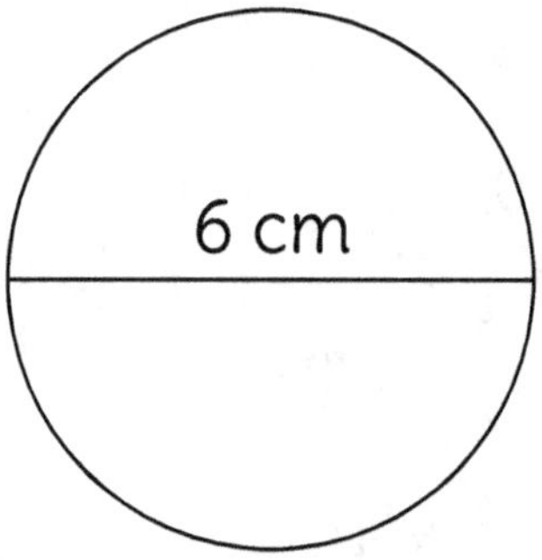

6 cm

____

5)

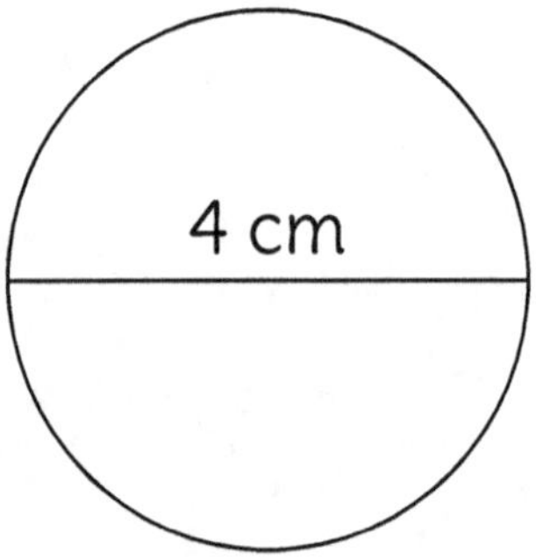

4 cm

____

6)

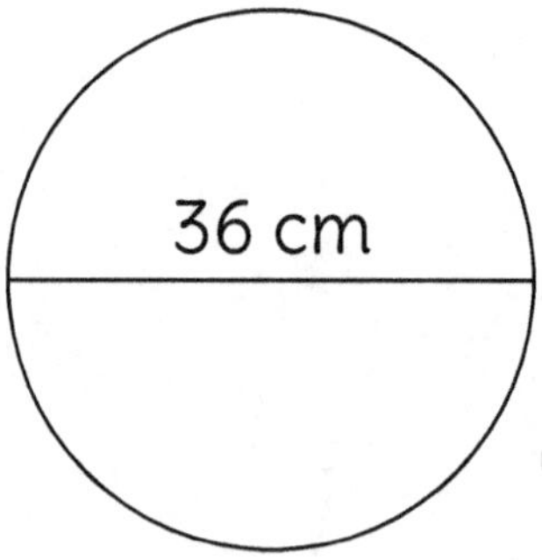

36 cm

____

7) 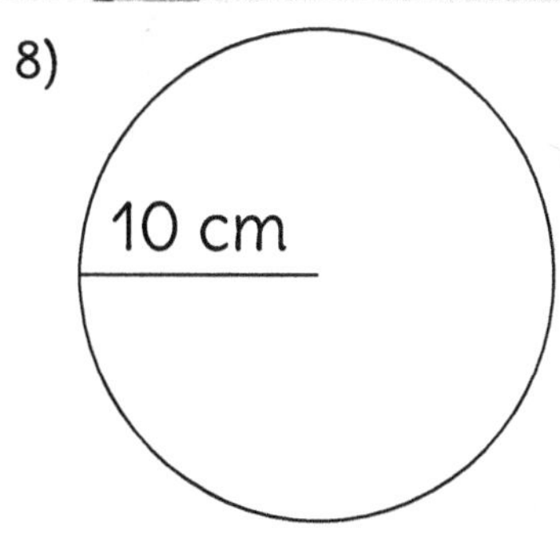

____

8)

____

9) 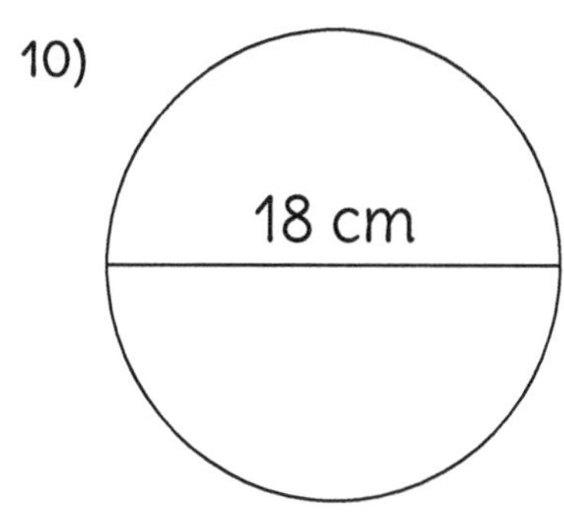

____

10)

____

11) 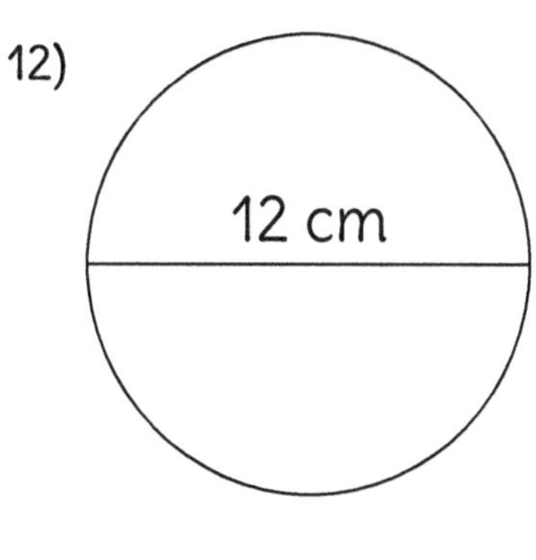

____

12)

____

13)

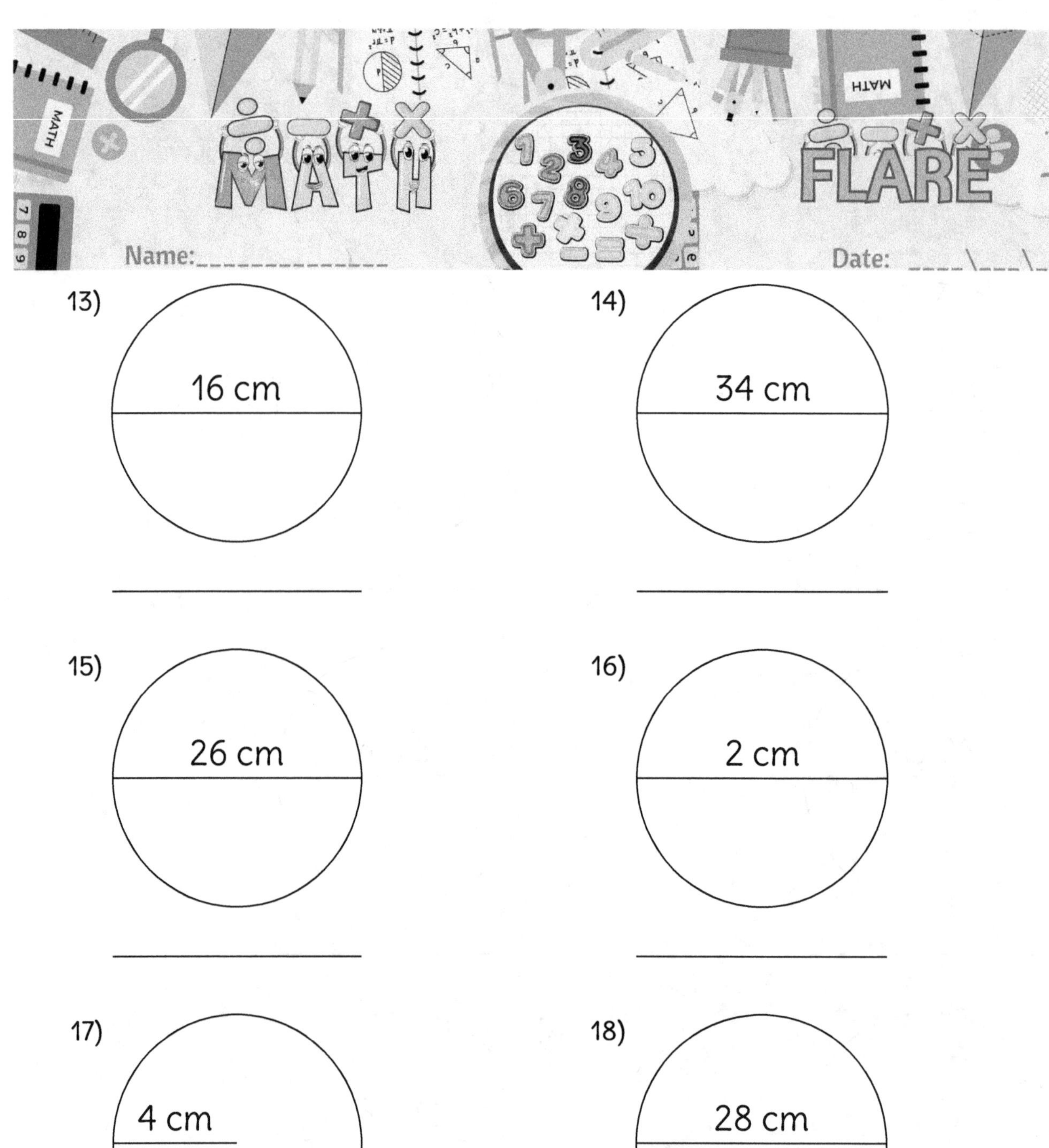

16 cm

____

14)

34 cm

____

15)

26 cm

____

16)

2 cm

____

17)

4 cm

____

18)

28 cm

____

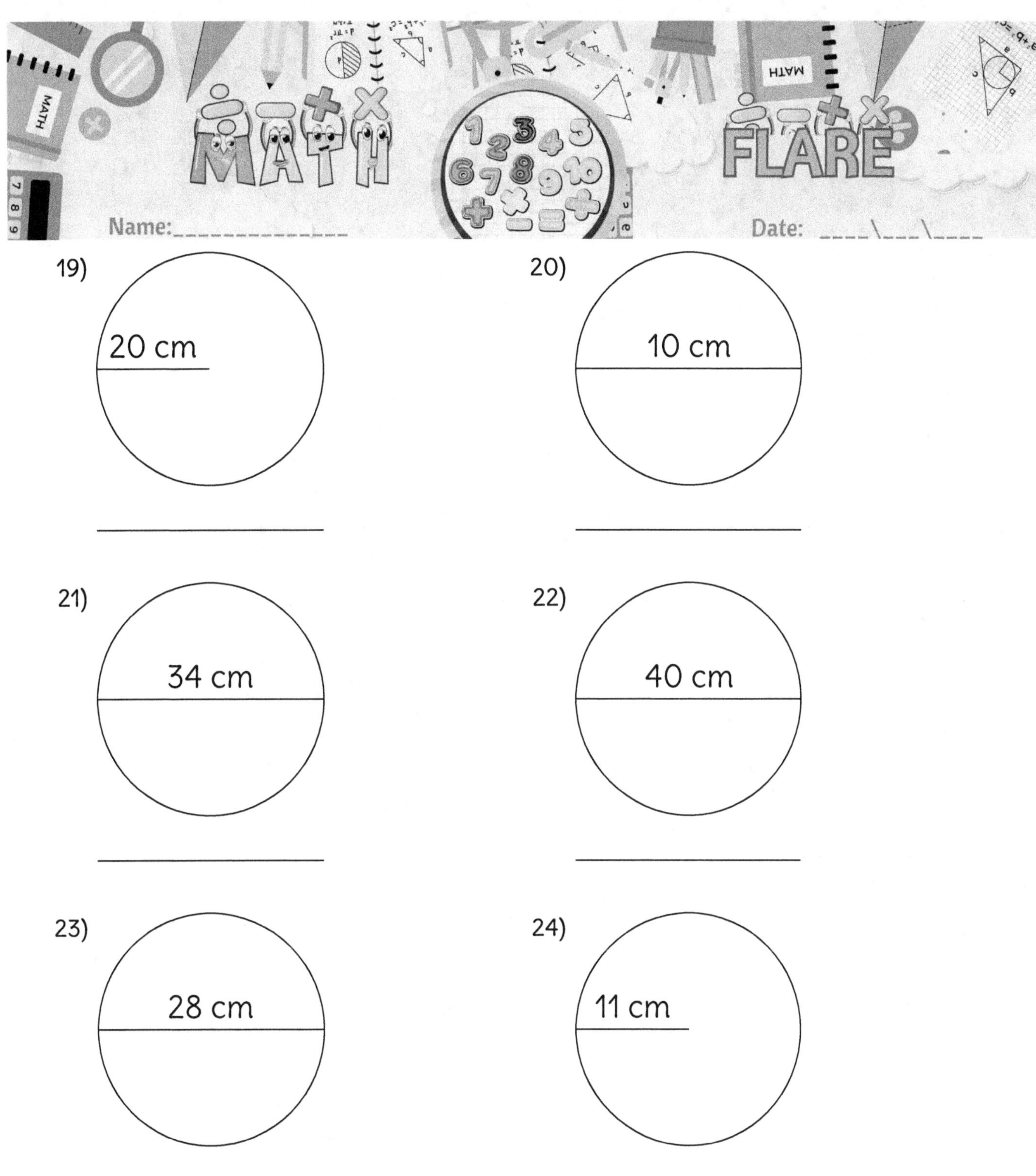
19)
20 cm

20)
10 cm

21)
34 cm

22)
40 cm

23)
28 cm

24)
11 cm

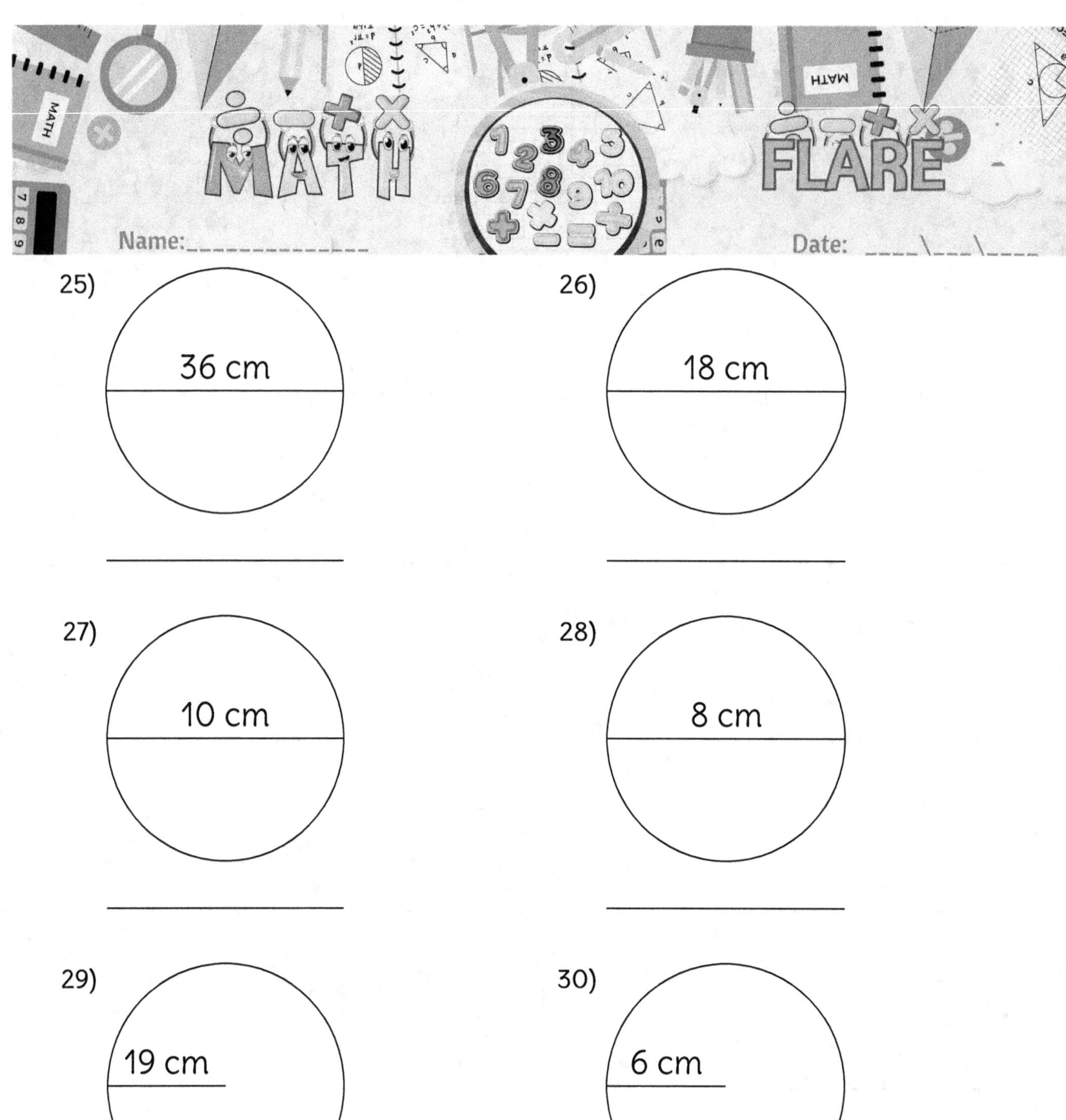

25)
36 cm
26)
18 cm
27)
10 cm
28)
8 cm
29)
19 cm
30)
6 cm

Chapter. 05

Unit Conversion

Metric Conversion
1 meter (m) = 100 centimeters (cm)
1 meter (m) = 1000 millimeters (mm)
1 kilometer (km) = 1000 meters (m)
1 hectare (ha) = 10000 square meters (m^2)
1 square meter (m^2) = 10000 square centimeters (cm^2)
1 cubic meter (m^3) = 1000 liters (L)

Weights and Measures
1 kilogram (kg) = 1000 grams (g)
1 liter (L) = 1000 milliliters (mL)
1 tonne (t) = 1000 kilograms (kg)
1 centimeter (cm) = 10 millimeters (mm)
1 gram (g) = 1000 milligrams (mg)
1 kilometer (km) = 100000 centimeters (cm)

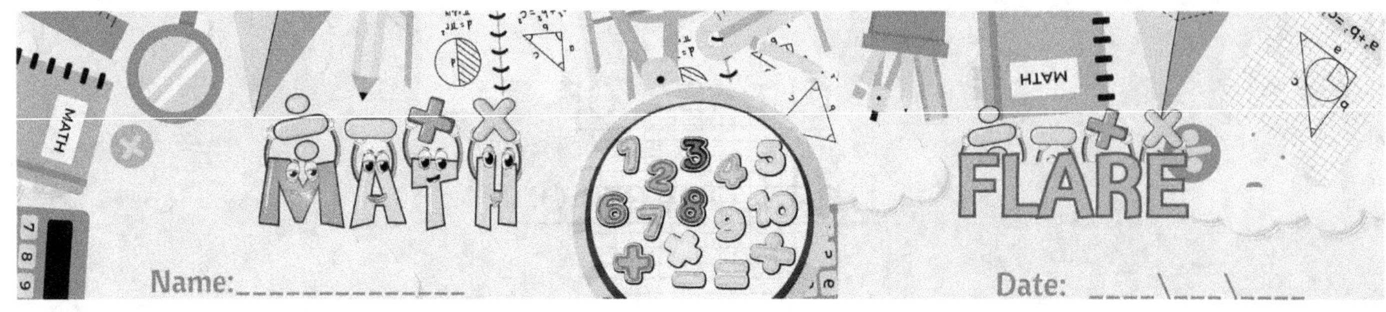

Metric Conversion

Convert the given measures.

1) 71 ft = _21.641_ m

2) 90 ft = __________ m

3) 57 ft = __________ m

4) 33 in = __________ m

5) 57 ft = __________ m

6) 88 ft = __________ m

7) 40 in = __________ m

8) 18 ft = __________ m

9) 76 in = __________ m

10) 14 in = __________ m

11) 56 ft = __________ m

12) 84 ft = __________ m

13) 35 in = __________ m

14) 77 in = __________ m

15) 10 in = __________ m

16) 97 ft = __________ m

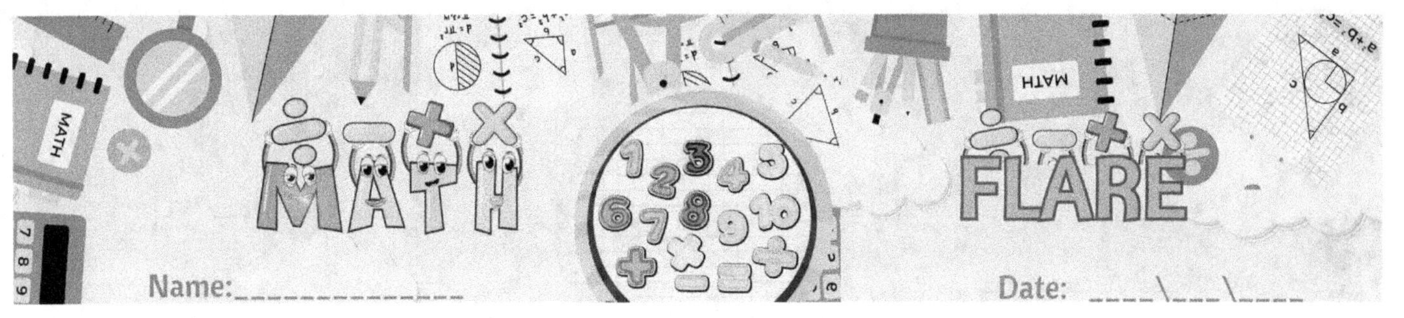

17) 37 in = _______________ m

18) 67 ft = _______________ m

19) 46 in = _______________ m

20) 72 ft = _______________ m

21) 53 in = _______________ m

22) 94 in = _______________ m

23) 64 in = _______________ m

24) 19 ft = _______________ m

25) 88 in = _______________ m

26) 27 ft = _______________ m

27) 93 in = _______________ m

28) 42 ft = _______________ m

29) 78 in = _______________ m

30) 14 in = _______________ m

31) 19 ft = _______________ m

32) 44 ft = _______________ m

33) 49 in = _______________ m

34) 68 ft = _______________ m

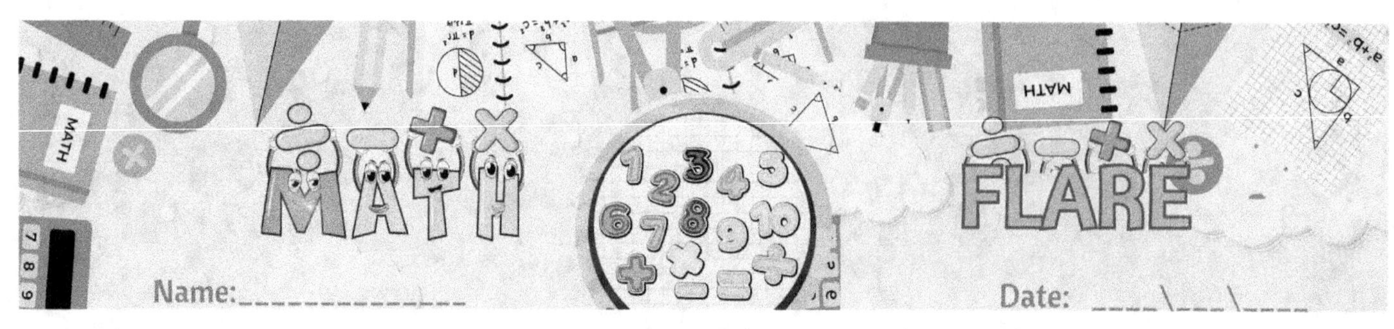

35) 75 ft = _______________ m 36) 65 in = _______________ m

37) 99 in = _______________ m 38) 50 ft = _______________ m

39) 43 in = _______________ m 40) 38 ft = _______________ m

41) 86 in = _______________ m 42) 18 in = _______________ m

43) 86 ft = _______________ m 44) 48 in = _______________ m

45) 63 ft = _______________ m 46) 52 ft = _______________ m

47) 52 ft = _______________ m 48) 65 ft = _______________ m

49) 72 ft = _______________ m 50) 63 in = _______________ m

51) 90 ft = _______________ m 52) 51 in = _______________ m

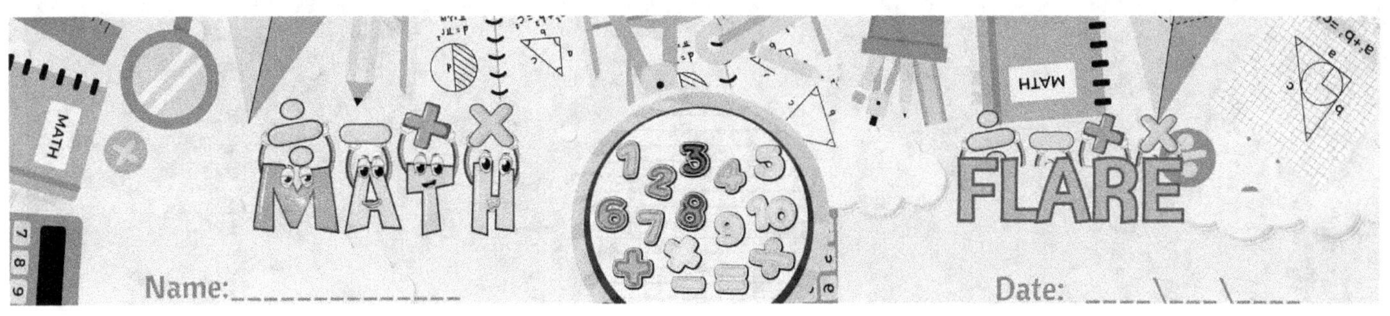

Name:____________________ Date: ____________

53) 94 ft = _______________ m

54) 43 in = _______________ m

55) 17 in = _______________ m

56) 75 ft = _______________ m

57) 36 in = _______________ m

58) 48 in = _______________ m

59) 45 ft = _______________ m

60) 40 ft = _______________ m

61) 94 ft = _______________ m

62) 97 in = _______________ m

63) 39 ft = _______________ m

64) 72 ft = _______________ m

65) 95 in = _______________ m

66) 22 in = _______________ m

67) 45 in = _______________ m

68) 66 in = _______________ m

69) 12 in = _______________ m

70) 44 in = _______________ m

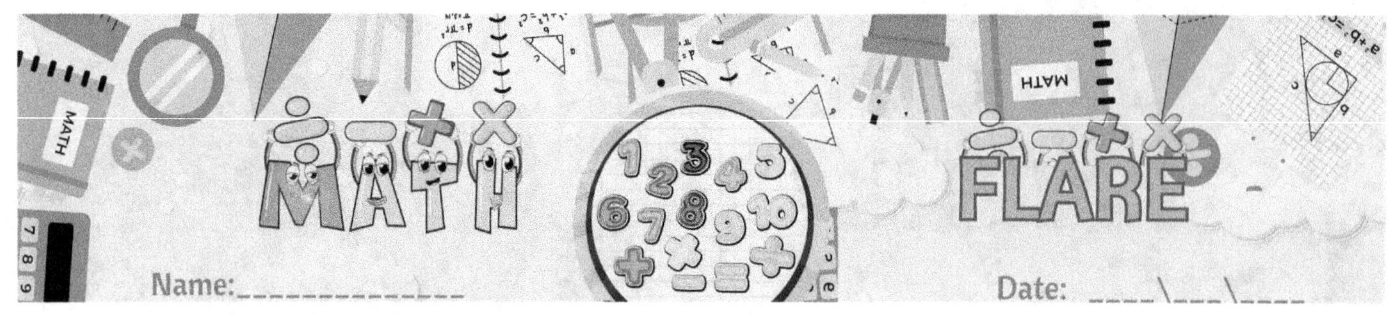

Metric Weights and Measures

Convert the given measures to new units.

1) 98 m = __0.098__ km

2) 87 L = __________ kL

3) 33 L = __________ kL

4) 18 L = __________ kL

5) 85 km = __________ m

6) 45 mL = __________ kL

7) 18 mL = __________ kL

8) 26 t = __________ kg

9) 56 g = __________ kg

10) 45 km = __________ m

11) 74 g = __________ t

12) 37 kg = __________ t

13) 69 m = __________ cm

14) 25 mL = __________ kL

15) 23 L = __________ kL

16) 66 kL = __________ L

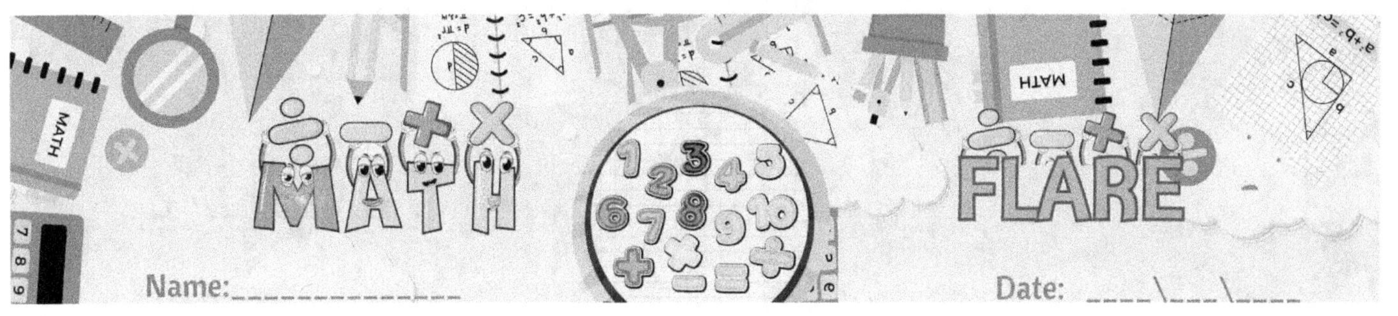

17) 49 t = _______________ kg

18) 16 m = _______________ km

19) 61 mL = _______________ L

20) 99 t = _______________ kg

21) 39 m = _______________ km

22) 61 kL = _______________ mL

23) 15 km = _______________ cm

24) 14 cm = _______________ km

25) 42 kg = _______________ t

26) 89 cm = _______________ m

27) 78 kg = _______________ g

28) 24 kg = _______________ t

29) 53 kL = _______________ L

30) 51 kL = _______________ L

31) 17 kg = _______________ t

32) 85 L = _______________ kL

33) 64 g = _______________ kg

34) 38 mL = _______________ L

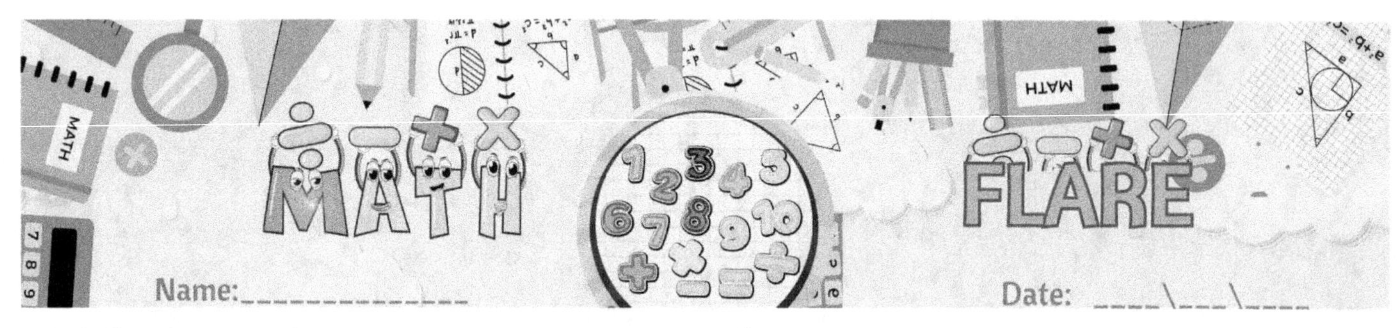

35) 65 m = _______________ km

36) 14 m = _______________ km

37) 28 cm = _______________ km

38) 86 kg = _______________ t

39) 58 kL = _______________ mL

40) 71 kL = _______________ L

41) 67 kL = _______________ L

42) 20 m = _______________ km

43) 91 kg = _______________ t

44) 98 t = _______________ kg

45) 64 km = _______________ cm

46) 67 g = _______________ t

47) 38 t = _______________ kg

48) 24 kg = _______________ g

49) 59 t = _______________ kg

50) 38 L = _______________ mL

51) 72 kL = _______________ mL

ANSWERS

Page 1: Multiplication: (3 x 3)

1. 327,894	2. 343,487	3. 279,380	4. 594,672	5. 216,916
6. 92,456	7. 33,792	8. 620,004	9. 242,852	10. 144,691
11. 370,300	12. 426,716	13. 276,340	14. 316,800	15. 389,272
16. 261,790	17. 120,000	18. 333,870	19. 321,048	20. 122,625
21. 92,852	22. 270,802	23. 628,992	24. 326,772	25. 48,180
26. 122,711	27. 677,844	28. 319,680	29. 432,900	30. 385,672
31. 164,400	32. 168,704	33. 224,208	34. 489,922	35. 166,254
36. 14,672				

Page 4: Multi Digit Multiplication

1. 11,362,810	2. 9,206,670	3. 9,257,408	4. 14,497,032
5. 5,444,660	6. 18,887,659	7. 51,774,360	8. 56,281,368
9. 12,478,991	10. 84,637,655	11. 6,563,025	12. 34,571,776
13. 43,196,413	14. 19,956,748	15. 81,184,510	16. 12,207,390
17. 25,408,705	18. 9,939,831	19. 12,992,238	20. 48,828,564
21. 45,151,434	22. 53,769,436	23. 19,916,318	24. 50,828,330
25. 31,246,320	26. 6,128,284	27. 22,407,156	28. 19,241,680
29. 38,493,306	30. 17,760,665	31. 28,878,496	32. 14,360,796
33. 17,275,940	34. 7,754,890	35. 37,441,581	36. 13,355,152

Page 8:   Long Division

1. 8,965.1	2. 17,076	3. 46,997.5	4. 8,100.3
5. 4,970.7	6. 17,549	7. 3,336	8. 22,568.7
9. 10,238	10. 8,937.7	11. 17,383.5	12. 6,308.1
13. 1,882.3	14. 24,651	15. 31,787.5	16. 4,312.6
17. 4,833.8	18. 7,796.2	19. 15,648.8	20. 10,594.8
21. 11,698	22. 4,979.2	23. 9,904.6	24. 2,974.6
25. 4,674.9	26. 40,019.5	27. 11,298.7	28. 5,361.9
29. 6,107.1	30. 2,621.3	31. 8,153	32. 30,068.3
33. 4,503.7	34. 19,293.8	35. 4,402	36. 10,514.5
37. 4,783.8	38. 7,370.6	39. 11,701.8	40. 24,955.7

Page 15:   Long Division: Remainders

1. 3,313 R3	2. 2,573 R8	3. 13,243 R5	4. 5,936 R0
5. 5,360 R0	6. 4,132 R5	7. 3,958 R12	8. 12,937 R2
9. 6,383 R6	10. 10,925 R4	11. 19,629 R2	12. 15,046 R5
13. 2,580 R0	14. 6,277 R4	15. 6,402 R2	16. 9,178 R5
17. 25,027 R1	18. 1,478 R4	19. 23,093 R1	20. 9,186 R7
21. 1,661 R7	22. 2,872 R16	23. 5,112 R6	24. 20,701 R2
25. 5,162 R13	26. 18,842 R3	27. 8,299 R1	28. 5,481 R3

Page 22:   Multiplying Decimals

1. 121.4256	2. 88.1454	3. 447.3945	4. 287.1777

5. 384.1596   6. 144.1174   7. 513.7392   8. 626.6120

9. 472.9921   10. 149.6764   11. 599.4412   12. 885.9604

13. 510.1889   14. 658.4031   15. 552.2762   16. 456.6405

17. 342.1362   18. 263.1846   19. 584.6400   20. 383.9040

21. 155.4336   22. 288.9428   23. 69.1385   24. 128.9156

25. 35.0750   26. 211.8194   27. 87.0144   28. 131.7536

29. 93.4830   30. 39.4295   31. 69.4328   32. 589.6800

33. 188.9559   34. 63.1454   35. 37.1168   36. 32.7248

37. 660.4633   38. 235.5936   39. 206.2800   40. 561.1528

41. 145.1177   42. 524.5760   43. 50.3475   44. 258.2088

45. 253.2607   46. 223.2395   47. 471.3510   48. 273.4032

49. 153.4158   50. 800.1116   51. 24.7640   52. 33.5064

53. 331.9680   54. 304.5726   55. 182.5520   56. 512.3593

57. 411.7680   58. 554.4000   59. 276.8920   60. 122.7660

61. 551.7413   62. 564.7190   63. 496.6542

Page 29: Dividing Decimals

1. 12.188   2. 5.267   3. 4.037   4. 11.138   5. 8.145

6. 9.68   7. 3.329   8. 3.475   9. 19.18   10. 9.325

11. 4.789   12. 5.92   13. 1.985   14. 4.539   15. 6.188

16. 9.088   17. 1.441   18. 3.525   19. 1.35   20. 47.3

21. 17.18   22. 1.18   23. 6.229   24. 1.08   25. 3.38

26. 1.565   27. 4.881   28. 7.582   29. 27.9   30. 14.967

31. 1.175   32. 15.467   33. 6.875   34. 2.671   35. 2.613

36. 7.155   37. 7.3   38. 10.125   39. 15.733   40. 1.053

41. 29.75   42. 5.138

Page 34: Multiplication Word Problems

1. 44   2. 90   3. 26   4. 39   5. 76   6. 72   7. 99

8. 198   9. 26   10. 240   11. 45   12. 135   13. 90   14. 119

15. 76   16. 78   17. 187   18. 80   19. 112   20. 39   21. 210

22. 221   23. 104   24. 84   25. 150   26. 238   27. 66   28. 50

29. 119   30. 160

Page 42: Division Word Problems

1. 97   2. 11   3. 34   4. 48   5. 65   6. 46   7. 47   8. 59

9. 41   10. 5   11. 75   12. 21   13. 10   14. 57   15. 60   16. 72

17. 12   18. 35   19. 46   20. 58   21. 94   22. 90   23. 29   24. 15

25. 45

Page 49: Using the Power of 10

1. 0.9   2. 110   3. 6,700   4. 0.06   5. 96,000

6. 73,000   7. 260   8. 0.98   9. 0.7   10. 4,000

11. 4,100   12. 0.21   13. 4,700   14. 0.91   15. 620

16. 0.93   17. 13,000   18. 52,000   19. 16,000   20. 9,200

21. 72,000   22. 8.1   23. 6,900   24. 5.7   25. 1,200

26. 0.01   27. 8.2   28. 24,000   29. 2,900   30. 0.95

31. 0.11   32. 0.5   33. 7,600   34. 0.04   35. 0.07

36. 0.34   37. 3.4   38. 8.5   39. 530   40. 0.77

41. 0.55   42. 14,000   43. 5.5   44. 670   45. 46,000

46. 6,400   47. 290   48. 9,600   49. 8.7   50. 3

51. 0.51   52. 0.97   53. 2,000   54. 200   55. 0.56

56. 0.09   57. 5.1   58. 440   59. 4   60. 710

61. 0.07   62. 6,200   63. 0.88   64. 69,000

Page 53: Place Value

1. 6 tens

2. 5 hundreds

3. 5 ten thousands

4. 4 ten millions

5. 9 tens

6. 1 hundred

7. 2 hundreds

8. 1 thousand

9. 4 ones

10. 8 thousands

11. 2 ten millions

12. 7 tens

13. 0 thousands

14. 8 tenths

15. 6 ten thousands

16. 1 thousand

17. 5 thousandths

18. 0 thousands

19. 0 tenths

20. 2 hundred thousands

21. 3 ones

22. 9 thousands

23. 4 tens

24. 2 ones

25. 2 thousandths

26. 7 tenths

27. 4 hundred thousands

28. 7 hundreds

29. 2 ten millions

30. 9 hundreds

31. 1 thousandth

32. 0 tens

33. 4 ten millions

34. 9 tenths

35. 1 ten million

36. 1 thousand

37. 0 hundredths

38. 2 ones

39. 2 ones

Page 58: Place Value and Expanded Notation

1. 175,596.19
2. 21,582,964
3. 67,521.630
4. 16,986.650
5. 9,336,281.3
6. 62,555,416
7. 800,078.57
8. 33,958,272
9. 74,613,631
10. 49,075,841
11. 551,680.52
12. 5,095,048.1
13. 121,788.73
14. 86,392.216
15. 932,635.62
16. 51,092.073
17. 77,888,503
18. 2,459,203.9
19. 9,784,726.6
20. 88,794.730
21. 510,190.00
22. 452,176.29
23. 89,772,716
24. 10,228,287
25. 59,557,313
26. 18,391.835
27. 365,458.31
28. 94,325,343
29. 19,128.700
30. 24,163.296
31. 15,336,297
32. 58,785,728
33. 799,232.82
34. 998,226.09
35. 256,949.17
36. 63,306,848
37. 412,680.00
38. 88,131,833
39. 83,009.771
40. 830,590.51

Page 64: Place Value and Expanded Notation

1. 8,684,690.5
2. 8,066,278.0
3. 911,158.81
4. 607,355.20

5. 78,435.739   6. 95,670.757   7. 99,103,503   8. 18,418.076

9. 183,102.26   10. 3,501,027.1   11. 55,523,671   12. 70,156,956

13. 702,989.01   14. 9,618,446.6   15. 40,784,925   16. 723,419.88

17. 31,810.247   18. 67,293.343   19. 57,429,336   20. 84,970,978

21. 36,009,585   22. 856,825.13   23. 248,295.73   24. 60,450,336

25. 43,739.544   26. 9,638,232.4   27. 7,102,719.8   28. 1,235,626.3

29. 706,972.99   30. 3,995,671.4   31. 19,824,074   32. 897,566.69

33. 41,582.267   34. 24,788.216   35. 1,194,782.6   36. 7,035,621.8

37. 541,017.47   38. 39,037,196   39. 31,792.546   40. 6,388,655.5

Page 74: Place Value and Expanded Notation

1. 1 hundred thousand + 9 ten thousands + 2 thousands + 8 hundreds + 8 tens + 3 ones + 3 tenths

2. 2 millions + 8 hundred thousands + 1 ten thousand + 2 thousands + 7 hundreds + 7 tens + 5 ones + 5 tenths

3. 8 hundred thousands + 6 ten thousands + 1 hundred + 5 tens + 1 one + 1 tenth + 6 hundredths

4. 8 ten thousands + 4 thousands + 1 hundred + 1 ten + 8 ones + 4 tenths + 2 hundredths + 7 thousandths

5. 6 millions + 8 hundred thousands + 6 ten thousands + 3 thousands + 9 hundreds + 6 tens + 2 ones + 4 tenths

6. 4 hundred thousands + 5 ten thousands + 1 thousand + 7 hundreds + 9 tens + 3 ones + 4 tenths

7. 8 ten millions + 8 millions + 4 hundred thousands + 8 ten thousands + 6 thousands + 8 hundreds + 2 tens + 6 ones

8. 8 millions + 3 hundred thousands + 7 ten thousands + 3 thousands + 8 hundreds + 8 tens + 1 one + 5 tenths

9. 6 hundred thousands + 9 ten thousands + 3 hundreds + 7 tens + 6 ones + 8 tenths + 3 hundredths

10. 5 ten thousands + 3 thousands + 3 hundreds + 5 tens + 2 ones + 9 tenths + 2 hundredths + 8 thousandths

11. 4 hundred thousands + 1 ten thousand + 4 thousands + 9 hundreds + 6 tens + 6 ones + 2 hundredths

12. 7 hundred thousands + 3 ten thousands + 9 thousands + 7 hundreds + 4 tens + 6 ones + 5 tenths + 5 hundredths

13. 4 millions + 7 ten thousands + 2 hundreds + 4 tens + 9 ones + 7 tenths

14. 9 millions + 8 hundred thousands + 3 thousands + 8 hundreds + 7 tens + 9 ones + 2 tenths

15. 5 ten thousands + 7 thousands + 4 tens + 9 ones + 4 tenths + 6 hundredths + 6 thousandths

16. 1 hundred thousand + 1 ten thousand + 1 thousand + 6 hundreds + 4 tens + 3 ones + 9 tenths + 2 hundredths

17. 6 millions + 5 hundred thousands + 8 ten thousands + 3 thousands + 3 hundreds + 2 tens + 8 tenths

18. 4 hundred thousands + 6 thousands + 6 hundreds + 5 tens + 5 ones + 4 tenths + 5 hundredths

19. 2 millions + 6 hundred thousands + 9 ten thousands + 9 thousands + 5 hundreds + 9 tens + 7 ones + 6 tenths

20. 8 millions + 2 hundred thousands + 5 thousands + 3 hundreds + 4 tens + 1 one + 5 tenths

21. 3 ten thousands + 4 thousands + 6 hundreds + 4 tens + 3 ones + 5 tenths + 5 hundredths + 9 thousandths

22. 9 ten millions + 6 millions + 7 hundred thousands + 4 ten thousands + 7 thousands + 2 hundreds + 4 tens

23. 4 ten millions + 7 millions + 7 hundred thousands + 2 ten thousands + 7 hundreds + 7 tens + 6 ones

24. 7 ten millions + 8 millions + 3 hundred thousands + 5 ten thousands + 3 thousands + 5 hundreds + 1 ten + 1 one

25. 2 millions + 5 hundred thousands + 1 ten thousand + 8 thousands + 6 hundreds + 1 ten + 9 ones + 8 tenths

26. 6 ten millions + 5 millions + 7 hundred thousands + 6 ten thousands + 7 thousands + 2 ones

27. 3 hundred thousands + 8 ten thousands + 5 thousands + 7 hundreds + 4 tens + 6 ones + 8 tenths + 9 hundredths

28. 5 ten millions + 5 millions + 5 hundred thousands + 1 ten thousand + 6 hundreds + 8 tens + 5 ones

29. 9 ten thousands + 4 thousands + 2 hundreds + 3 tens + 6 ones + 6 tenths + 4 hundredths + 1 thousandth

30. 7 ten thousands + 4 hundreds + 2 tens + 8 ones + 7 tenths + 6 thousandths

31. 2 hundred thousands + 8 ten thousands + 2 thousands + 4 hundreds + 2 ones + 4 tenths + 1 hundredth

32. 9 ten thousands + 2 thousands + 7 hundreds + 7 tens + 3 ones + 5 hundredths

33. 4 hundred thousands + 5 ten thousands + 5 thousands + 7 ones + 9 tenths + 7 hundredths

34. 9 hundred thousands + 3 ten thousands + 5 thousands + 4 hundreds + 2 tens + 7 ones + 8 tenths

35. 7 millions + 5 hundred thousands + 6 ten thousands + 8 thousands + 2 hundreds + 6 tens + 4 ones + 8 tenths

36. 1 million + 7 hundred thousands + 8 ten thousands + 8 thousands + 1 hundred + 8 tens + 3 ones

37. 9 ten millions + 9 millions + 6 hundred thousands + 6 ten thousands + 7 thousands + 3 hundreds + 9 tens + 6 ones

38. 4 millions + 7 ten thousands + 1 thousand + 1 hundred + 1 ten + 4 ones + 4 tenths

39. 9 hundred thousands + 1 ten thousand + 8 thousands + 1 hundred + 7 ones + 1 tenth + 1 hundredth

Page 82: Lowest Common Multiple

1. 56	2. 56	3. 8	4. 30	5. 35	6. 72	7. 12	8. 6
9. 40	10. 70	11. 72	12. 45	13. 40	14. 45	15. 4	16. 15
17. 15	18. 30	19. 10	20. 30	21. 28	22. 24	23. 8	24. 70
25. 20	26. 9	27. 6	28. 42	29. 14	30. 21	31. 35	32. 90
33. 40	34. 36	35. 10	36. 8	37. 30	38. 24	39. 28	40. 21
41. 6	42. 18	43. 20	44. 12	45. 8	46. 4	47. 63	

Page 90:   Equivalent Fractions

1. 4   2. 8   3. 152   4. 5   5. 2   6. 15   7. 17

8. 80   9. 5   10. 6   11. 2   12. 14   13. 13   14. 40

15. 14   16. 24   17. 10   18. 75   19. 3   20. 16   21. 6

22. 6   23. 2   24. 11   25. 8   26. 5   27. 80   28. 7

29. 15   30. 18   31. 5   32. 14   33. 80   34. 13   35. 150

36. 60   37. 2   38. 7   39. 1   40. 90   41. 36   42. 85

43. 1   44. 5   45. 14   46. 81   47. 5   48. 36   49. 19

50. 16

Page 95:   Fractions Addition: Uncommon Denominator

1. 31/44   2. 7/10   3. 23/30   4. 58/119   5. 38/45

6. 9/20   7. 33/52   8. 5/8   9. 5/6   10. 50/57

11. 7/24   12. 10/21   13. 55/76   14. 49/130   15. 1/2

16. 31/65   17. 9/14   18. 25/28   19. 163/180   20. 107/126

21. 36/77   22. 14/15   23. 8/9   24. 11/15   25. 4/5

26. 5/16   27. 35/44   28. 9/10   29. 5/6   30. 1/2

31. 15/112   32. 77/221   33. 19/40   34. 29/66   35. 13/18

36. 3/4   37. 8/15   38. 61/63   39. 31/39   40. 73/114

41. 5/12   42. 81/95   43. 89/306   44. 4/5   45. 37/48

46. 3/4   47. 3/4   48. 17/21   49. 19/60   50. 89/91

51. 9/16   52. 45/56   53. 3/5   54. 25/52   55. 21/68

56. 2/3   57. 25/34   58. 23/45

Page 100:   Fractions Subtraction: (Uncommon Denominator)

1. 3/34   2. 122/221   3. 23/90   4. 12/221   5. 179/240

6. 1/10   7. 34/143   8. 1/21   9. 1/7   10. 53/88

11. 13/20   12. 5/18   13. 7/18   14. 25/266   15. 7/38

16. 1/6   17. 13/34   18. 1/48   19. 7/15   20. 36/95

21. 15/52   22. 13/24   23. 1/6   24. 1/5   25. 206/255

26. 27/40   27. 23/78   28. 5/14   29. 191/221   30. 4/21

31. 1/10   32. 1/10   33. 41/117   34. 2/15   35. 7/12

36. 31/247   37. 2/5   38. 5/21   39. 1/9   40. 1/8

41. 6/65   42. 47/65   43. 1/85   44. 1/6   45. 13/45

46. 5/12   47. 58/133   48. 16/33   49. 1/6   50. 3/8

51. 26/95   52. 7/36   53. 13/45   54. 2/9   55. 14/209

56. 1/35

Page 105:   Fractions Multiplication

1. 4/15   2. 1/9   3. 40/99   4. 1/12   5. 1/3

6. 3/16   7. 4/33   8. 4/27   9. 7/16   10. 5/36

11. 2/63   12. 2/21   13. 1/9   14. 8/33   15. 16/45

16. 1/16   17. 9/22   18. 2/49   19. 5/12   20. 1/5

21. 1/16   22. 3/8   23. 5/72   24. 2/9   25. 3/22

26. 1/16   27. 1/15   28. 5/11   29. 1/42   30. 16/27

31. 1/30   32. 8/27   33. 11/24   34. 1/8   35. 1/7

36. 16/33   37. 8/25   38. 3/20   39. 1/8   40. 25/56

41. 4/11   42. 4/9   43. 21/100   44. 25/49   45. 3/5

46. 5/24

Page 109: Fractions Division

1. 11/45   2. 1 1/3   3. 2/3   4. 1 3/22   5. 1 3/25   6. 1 5/6

7. 1/5   8. 1/10   9. 1 10/11   10. 4/9   11. 1 5/16   12. 2

13. 1/4   14. 2   15. 5/8   16. 1 1/2   17. 3   18. 1/4

19. 4/9   20. 7/15   21. 1 3/4   22. 1 3/77   23. 1   24. 2 1/3

25. 3   26. 3/10   27. 11/18   28. 25/48   29. 40/63   30. 1 2/7

31. 1 3/5   32. 4/9   33. 1 1/2   34. 6 7/8   35. 9/28   36. 1/4

37. 1/6   38. 15/22   39. 2 5/36   40. 1 1/5   41. 1 1/8   42. 5/6

43. 1   44. 5/24   45. 2 1/24   46. 2

Page 113: Fractions Addition Word Problems

1. 5/6   2. 38/45   3. 6/7   4. 3/4   5. 4/8   6. 17/30

7. 19/28   8. 11/15   9. 3/5   10. 17/18   11. 5/6   12. 8/9

13. 7/12   14. 41/45   15. 1   16. 5/6   17. 19/21   18. 8/15

19. 13/21   20. 11/15   21. 11/14   22. 2/3   23. 3/4   24. 9/20

25. 7/10   26. 5/6   27. 24/35   28. 7/9   29. 51/56   30. 23/24

Page 123: Fractions Subtraction Word Problems

1. 1/15   2. 1/9   3. 5/12   4. 1/8   5. 1/18   6. 5/12

7. 1/6   8. 23/35   9. 1/20   10. 3/10   11. 11/24   12. 1/3

13. 37/72   14. 3/14   15. 5/14   16. 3/10   17. 2/15   18. 1/2

19. 3/10   20. 3/7   21. 1/6   22. 23/40   23. 17/42   24. 3/8

25. 2/5   26. 1/6   27. 1/12   28. 23/36   29. 2/5   30. 7/24

Page 133:   Area and Perimeter: Rectangles and Triangles

1. P=18 A=15.59   2. P=32 A=60   3. P=64 A=256

4. P=28 A=36.68   5. P=35 A=50   6. P=24 A=27.71

7. P=42 A=82.5   8. P=23 A=24   9. P=49 A=105

10. P=48 A=110.85   11. P=28 A=36   12. P=24 A=27.71

13. P=48 A=110.85   14. P=15 A=10.82   15. P=40 A=99

16. P=28 A=36.68   17. P=22 A=22.26   18. P=43 A=78

19. P=33 A=50.04   20. P=46 A=91   21. P=41 A=71.5

22. P=51 A=125.12   23. P=34 A=50   24. P=21 A=21.22

25. P=44 A=84   26. P=46 A=90   27. P=39 A=66

28. P=48 A=97.5   29. P=23 A=25.16   30. P=46 A=132

31. P=32 A=64   32. P=38 A=90   33. P=48 A=97.5

34. P=55 A=127.5   35. P=18 A=15.59   36. P=31 A=45.18

37. P=48 A=97.5   38. P=22 A=20   39. P=30 A=40

40. P=48 A=110.85   41. P=22 A=22.26   42. P=28 A=36.68

43. P=36 A=80   44. P=34 A=48   45. P=43 A=77

46. P=25 A=28   47. P=41 A=80.6   48. P=23 A=25.16

Page 145: Circumference

1. C=69.08 cm   2. C=119.32 cm   3. C=75.36 cm

4. C=18.84 cm   5. C=12.56 cm   6. C=113.04 cm

7. C=94.20 cm   8. C=62.80 cm   9. C=100.48 cm

10. C=56.52 cm   11. C=43.96 cm   12. C=37.68 cm

13. C=50.24 cm   14. C=106.76 cm   15. C=81.64 cm

16. C=6.28 cm   17. C=25.12 cm   18. C=87.92 cm

19. C=125.60 cm   20. C=31.40 cm   21. C=106.76 cm

22. C=125.60 cm   23. C=87.92 cm   24. C=69.08 cm

25. C=113.04 cm   26. C=56.52 cm   27. C=31.40 cm

28. C=25.12 cm   29. C=119.32 cm   30. C=37.68 cm

Page 150: Metric Conversion

1. 21.641   2. 27.432   3. 17.374   4. 0.838   5. 17.374

6. 26.822   7. 1.016   8. 5.486   9. 1.930   10. 0.356

11. 17.069   12. 25.603   13. 0.889   14. 1.956   15. 0.254

16. 29.566   17. 0.940   18. 20.422   19. 1.168   20. 21.946

21. 1.346   22. 2.388   23. 1.626   24. 5.791   25. 2.235

26. 8.230   27. 2.362   28. 12.802   29. 1.981   30. 0.356

31. 5.791   32. 13.411   33. 1.245   34. 20.726   35. 22.860

36. 1.651   37. 2.515   38. 15.240   39. 1.092   40. 11.582

41. 2.184   42. 0.457   43. 26.213   44. 1.219   45. 19.202

46. 15.850 47. 15.850 48. 19.812 49. 21.946 50. 1.600

51. 27.432 52. 1.295 53. 28.651 54. 1.092 55. 0.432

56. 22.860 57. 0.914 58. 1.219 59. 13.716 60. 12.192

61. 28.651 62. 2.464 63. 11.887 64. 21.946 65. 2.413

66. 0.559 67. 1.143 68. 1.676 69. 0.305 70. 1.118

Page 154: Metric Weights and Measures

1. 0.098 2. 0.087 3. 0.033 4. 0.018

5. 85,000 6. 0.000045 7. 0.000018 8. 26,000

9. 0.056 10. 45,000 11. 0.000074 12. 0.037

13. 6,900 14. 0.000025 15. 0.023 16. 66,000

17. 49,000 18. 0.016 19. 0.061 20. 99,000

21. 0.039 22. 61,000,000 23. 1,500,000 24. 0.00014

25. 0.042 26. 0.89 27. 78,000 28. 0.024

29. 53,000 30. 51,000 31. 0.017 32. 0.085

33. 0.064 34. 0.038 35. 0.065 36. 0.014

37. 0.00028 38. 0.086 39. 58,000,000 40. 71,000

41. 67,000 42. 0.020 43. 0.091 44. 98,000

45. 6,400,000 46. 0.000067 47. 38,000 48. 24,000

49. 59,000 50. 38,000 51. 72,000,000